P9-DHI-198

Reading Skills

Grade 3

Harcourt Family Learning™

FLASH KIDS and the distinctive Flash Kids logo are registered trademarks of Barnes & Noble Booksellers, Inc.
Harcourt Family Learning and Design is a trademark of Harcourt, Inc.

© 2004 Flash Kids
Adapted from *Comprehension Skills Complete Classroom Library*
by Linda Ward Beech, Tara McCarthy, and Donna Townsend
© 2001 Harcourt Achieve
Licensed under special arrangement with Harcourt Achieve.

All rights reserved. No part of this publication may be reproduced, stored in a retrieval system,
or transmitted in any form or by any means (including electronic, mechanical, photocopying,
recording, or otherwise) without prior written permission from the publisher.

For more information, please visit flashkids.com
Please submit all inquiries to Flashkids@sterlingpublishing.com

ISBN 978-1-4114-0115-0

Manufactured in China

Lot #:
40 42 44 46 45 43 41
11/18

Illustrator: Hector Borlasca

FlashKids
New York

Dear Parent,

The ability to read well is an important part of your child's development. This book is designed to help your child become a better reader. The wide range of high-interest stories will hold your child's attention and help develop his or her proficiency in reading. Each of the six units focuses on a different reading comprehension skill: finding facts, detecting a sequence, learning new vocabulary through context, identifying the main idea, drawing conclusions, and making inferences. Mastering these skills will ensure that your child has the necessary tools needed for a lifetime love of reading.

Unit 1 contains activities to fine-tune your child's ability to spot facts in a story—a necessary skill for understanding a reading selection. This unit is filled with stories to test your child's understanding of how to identify facts in a story. The focus is on specific details that tell who, what, when, where, and how.

Reading for sequence means identifying the order of events in a story or the steps in a process, and understanding the relationship of one event or step to other events or steps. Unit 2 contains stories that will test your child's understanding of the order of events in a story.

Unit 3 teaches your child how to use context to learn new words. When practicing using context, your child must use all the words in a reading selection to understand the unfamiliar words. This important skill helps a reader understand words and concepts by learning how language is used to express meaning. Mastering this skill ensures that your child will become a successful independent reader.

One of the keys to learning to read well is being able to differentiate between the main point of a reading selection and the supporting details. Unit 4 will help your child learn to recognize the main idea of a story.

Drawing a conclusion is a complex reading skill because a conclusion is not stated in a reading selection. Your child must learn to put together the details from the information as if they were clues to a puzzle. The conclusion must be supported by the details in the reading selection. Unit 5 contains stories to help your child learn to draw conclusions about the passages in the book.

To make an inference, your child must consider all the facts in a reading selection. Then he or she must put together those facts and what is already known to make a reasonable inference about something that is not stated in the selection. Making an inference requires the reader to go beyond the information in the text. Unit 6 will help your child learn how to make inferences.

To help your child get the most from this workbook, encourage your child to read each reading selection slowly and carefully. Explain the purpose of each unit to your child so that he or she has a better understanding of how it will help his or her reading skills. There's an answer key at the end of this workbook. Your child can check the answer key to see which questions he or she got right and wrong. Go back to the questions your child answered incorrectly and go over them again to see why he or she picked the incorrect answer. Completing the activities in this workbook will get your child on the right track to becoming an excellent reader. Continue your child's educational development at home with these fun activities:

- Enlist your child's help when writing grocery lists.
- When preparing a meal, have your child read the recipe aloud.
- Provide entertaining reading selections for your child. Have a discussion about what he or she has read.
- Instead of reading a bedtime story to your child, have your child read a bedtime story to you!
- Write down the directions to a project, such as a gardening project or an arts and crafts project, for your child to read.
- Give your child a fun reading passage and ask him or her to draw a picture about it.
- Ask your child to read road signs and billboards that you encounter during car trips.
- Leave cute notes on the refrigerator or your child's pillow.
- Have your child write and mail a letter to a loved one.
- Ask your child to read the directions for a board game, and then play the game together.
- Bring your child to the library or bookstore so that he or she can choose which great book to read next.

Table of Contents

4

What Are Facts?

Facts are sometimes called details. They are small bits of information. Facts are in true stories, such as those in the newspaper. There are facts in stories that people make up, too.

How to Read for Facts

You can find facts by asking yourself questions. Ask *who*, and your answer will be a fact about a person. Ask *what*, and your answer will be a fact about a thing. Ask *where*, and your answer will be a fact about a place. Ask *when*, and your answer will be a fact about a time. Ask *how many* or *how much*, and your answer will be a fact about a number or an amount.

Try It!

Read this story and look for facts as you read. Ask yourself *what* and *where*.

  Coober Pedy

Opals are stones that sparkle with many colors. Some of the most beautiful opals come from a town in South Australia. This town is called Coober Pedy. Opals were first found there in 1915. People like to visit this town. They come to buy opals and to see the unusual buildings. Coober Pedy gets very hot in the summer, so most people build their homes underground. In this way the homes stay cool in the summer and warm in the winter. Tourists can stay in an underground hotel.

Did you find these facts when you read the story? Write the facts on the lines below.

• What are opals?

Fact: _____

• Where is Coober Pedy?

Fact: _____

Practice Finding Facts

Below are some practice questions. The first two are already answered. You can do the third one on your own.

B __ **1.** When were opals first found at Coober Pedy?
     A. in 1991   **C.** in summer
     B. in 1915   **D.** in winter

Look at the question and answers again. The word *when* is asking for a time. Reread the story and look for times. Find the sentence that says, "Opals were first found there in 1915." So the correct answer is **B**.

C __ **2.** Tourists like to visit Coober Pedy
     A. to swim   **C.** to buy opals
     B. to dig   **D.** to learn to cook

Look at the question. It has the words *tourists like to visit*. Look for these words in the story. You will find this sentence: "People like to visit this town." Read the next sentence. It says, "They come to buy opals and to see the unusual buildings." The correct answer is **C**.

Now it's your turn to practice. Answer the next question. Write the letter of the correct answer on the line.

_____ **3.** Where can tourists stay?
     A. in a camp   **C.** in an apartment
     B. in a house   **D.** in an underground hotel

Read each story. After each story you will answer questions about the facts in the story. Remember, a fact is something that you know is true.

Secret Sharks

Most people think of sharks as the ones they see in the movies. These "movie stars" are usually the great white sharks. However, the great whites are just one of about 350 kinds of sharks. There are some sharks that have never been seen alive. They live deep in the ocean. They are like the sharks that lived 300 million years ago.

One example is the goblin shark. It lives hundreds of feet under the sea. Scientists do not believe that it could live if it came to the ocean surface. People in Japan have built a small submarine to learn more about goblin sharks.

Another unusual shark is the megamouth. *Mega* means large and strong. One megamouth that scientists have seen was 15 feet long. Its mouth was 4 feet long.

_____ 1. The sharks usually seen in movies are
      A. gray sharks   **C.** megamouth sharks
      B. goblin sharks   **D.** great white sharks

_____ 2. How many kinds of sharks are there?
      A. about 300   **C.** about 4,500
      B. about 15   **D.** about 350

_____ 3. The goblin shark will be studied using a
      A. submarine   **C.** library
      B. telescope   **D.** museum

_____ 4. *Mega* means large and
      A. mean   **C.** strong
      B. rare   **D.** hungry

_____ 5. The mouth of one megamouth was about
      A. 3 feet long   **C.** 15 feet long
      B. 4 feet long   **D.** 60 feet long

Scientists are trying to learn more about other unusual sharks. One is the frilled shark. This creature has a body like an eel. It has frills on its neck. Scientists want to know what the frilled shark eats. They think it may eat squid.

There are many interesting kinds of small sharks, too. The cookie-cutter shark is only 16 inches long, but it has very large teeth. This shark also has strong lips. It holds a larger fish with its lips while it scoops out big bites.

Many small sharks hunt together. This way they can kill fish much larger than themselves. One kind of shark that does this is the cigar shark. You can probably guess how this shark got its name. It is the size and shape of a cigar. It is even small enough for you to hold in your hand!

_____ **6.** Scientists are studying
    A. large sharks   **C.** unusual sharks
    B. unkind sharks   **D.** common sharks

_____ **7.** The shark that looks like an eel is the
    A. cigar shark   **C.** eel shark
    B. goblin shark   **D.** frilled shark

_____ **8.** The cookie-cutter shark is
    A. little   **C.** tasty
    B. huge   **D.** fishy

_____ **9.** The cookie-cutter shark has strong
    A. cookies   **C.** eyes
    B. fins   **D.** lips

_____ **10.** One shark that hunts in groups is the
    A. goblin shark   **C.** frilled shark
    B. cigar shark   **D.** ghost shark

The Sound Machine's Deaf Inventor

Thomas Edison was one of the greatest inventors of all time. One of his best-known works was the phonograph. He built it in 1877. It was the first machine to record and play sound. Any inventor of this sound machine could be called great. For Edison, it was a very great deed. That's because he was partly deaf.

When Tom was a teen, he worked on a train. One day he was late for work. He ran for the train just as it was pulling out of the station. The conductor tried to help the boy. He grabbed Tom by the ears and pulled him up. "I felt something snap inside my head," Edison said later. From that point on, he grew more and more deaf.

_____ **1.** Thomas Edison was a great
    A. doctor   **C.** inventor
    B. writer   **D.** president

_____ **2.** One of Edison's best-known works was the
    A. telephone   **C.** television
    B. phonograph   **D.** photograph

_____ **3.** The phonograph was built in
    A. 1887   **C.** 1877
    B. 1787   **D.** 1777

_____ **4.** Edison was
    A. totally blind   **C.** partly blind
    B. totally deaf   **D.** partly deaf

_____ **5.** Tom was hurt when his ears were pulled by a
    A. teacher   **C.** singer
    B. conductor   **D.** bully

Despite his hearing loss, Edison went on to invent many things. His favorite was the phonograph. Edison tested it once it was built. He spoke into the mouth of the machine. He said, "Mary had a little lamb." The machine played back his words.

How could Edison build a sound machine if he was deaf? He had a trick. He pressed his ear up to the machine to feel it vibrate.

Edison could have had an operation so he could hear again, but he chose not to. He said that being deaf helped him. He said it let him think better. Outside noises did not distract him at work. That was another part of his genius!

_____ **6.** The phonograph was Edison's
    A. only invention   **C.** last invention
    B. first invention   **D.** favorite invention

_____ **7.** Edison's phonograph
    A. did not work   **C.** made words louder
    B. helped Mary   **D.** repeated his words

_____ **8.** Edison could hear by pressing his ear to
    A. a paper cup   **C.** a hearing aid
    B. another person   **D.** the phonograph

_____ **9.** Edison did not have an ear operation because he
    A. had no choice   **C.** was afraid
    B. chose not to   **D.** was too busy

_____ **10.** Edison said that being deaf
    A. hurt him   **C.** made him tired
    B. annoyed him   **D.** aided him

The Oldest Toy

One of the very first toys was simple and round. It was a ball. The first balls were just rocks that were round and smooth. People liked kicking rocks to see how far the rocks would go. They also threw rocks to see if they could hit certain things with them.

Bowling was first played thousands of years ago in Egypt. A ball made of rock was rolled through a short tunnel. People tried to knock down the nine rock pieces at the other end of the tunnel.

Later bowling was played in Germany. At first people used a stone ball and one wooden pin. Then they used a ball made of wood. The number of pins also changed. Sometimes people used three pins. Other times people used as many as 17 pins.

_____ **1.** One of the very first toys was
  A. round   **C.** square
  B. sharp   **D.** flat

_____ **2.** People liked kicking rocks to see how
  A. soft they were   **C.** high they would go
  B. hard they were   **D.** far they would go

_____ **3.** The first bowling game was played
  A. in Egypt   **C.** in the United States
  B. in Germany   **D.** with one wooden pin

_____ **4.** In Egypt, a rock ball was rolled through a
  A. field   **C.** tunnel
  B. street   **D.** sidewalk

_____ **5.** At first in Germany people used
  A. three pins   **C.** one wooden pin
  B. 17 pins   **D.** 100 pins

Native Americans made up games that used balls. Some of them played a game that was like basketball. They even had a ball made of rubber. They got the rubber from the trees where they lived.

Handball games started in Europe. Children liked to bounce small balls made of animal skin against the sides of buildings. They especially liked the high stone walls of churches. Later people started hitting the ball to each other over a net. At first they used only their hands. Then they began to wrap their hands with string. They also added a stick. The game of tennis started from the game of handball.

_____ **6.** Some Native Americans had a ball that
      A. didn't bounce   **C.** they hit with a bat
      B. fell apart   **D.** was made of rubber

_____ **7.** Rubber comes from
      A. rivers   **C.** animal skins
      B. trees   **D.** the ground

_____ **8.** Handball was first played in
      A. prisons   **C.** Europe
      B. Japan   **D.** churches

_____ **9.** People first hit balls over nets with their
      A. gloves   **C.** hands
      B. feet   **D.** shoes

_____ **10.** Tennis came from the game of
      A. handball   **C.** bowling
      B. basketball   **D.** skin ball

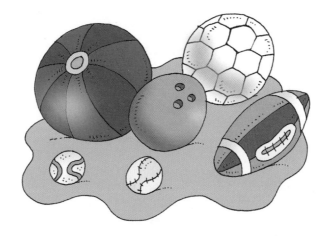

Save the Turkeys!

Turkeys are interesting birds. They don't take off and fly smoothly like other birds. Turkeys take off like helicopters. They go almost straight up and can fly fast. One wild turkey was timed flying at 55 miles per hour.

Turkeys differ from most birds in other ways, too. Male turkeys have snoods and wattles. The snood is a flap of skin above the beak. It can grow to be 5 inches long. Male turkeys use their snoods to attract females.

A turkey's wattle is the bumpy skin on his neck. It can grow very large. It can also turn from red to white and back again. Some people think that this happens when the turkey wants to send a message. He may be trying to attract a female. He might be sending a signal to another male that says, "Stay away!"

_____ **1.** When a turkey takes off, it flies
    A. slowly   **C.** straight up
    B. smoothly   **D.** near the ground

_____ **2.** One turkey was timed flying
    A. 5 feet per hour   **C.** 10 miles per hour
    B. 15 feet per hour   **D.** 55 miles per hour

_____ **3.** A turkey's snood can be found
    A. on its back   **C.** under the wing
    B. above the beak   **D.** above the eye

_____ **4.** A wattle is part of the turkey's
    A. neck   **C.** foot
    B. feathers   **D.** beak

_____ **5.** A turkey's wattle can turn from red to
    A. black   **C.** white
    B. blue   **D.** brown

Turkeys were once threatened birds. Wild turkeys lived in the woods. People cut down the woods to make roads, towns, and farms. The turkeys had no place to live. People liked to eat turkeys, so hunters killed many of these birds. By the 1900s the number of turkeys in America had dropped. Very few were left.

Leaders in each state knew that something had to be done. They passed laws to solve the problem. Some laws placed limits on the number of turkeys that hunters could kill. Also, laws allowed some turkeys to be moved to areas where others had vanished. The new laws helped turkeys, and people learned that passing laws to help them is one way to take care of wild animals.

_____ **6.** As people changed the land, wild turkeys
     A. flew straight up   **C.** lost their homes
     B. lived in towns   **D.** enjoyed people

_____ **7.** Hunters killed many turkeys for
     A. food   **C.** wattles
     B. beaks   **D.** feathers

_____ **8.** The turkeys were finally helped by
     A. experts   **C.** lawmakers
     B. hunters   **D.** soldiers

_____ **9.** Turkeys were saved by being moved to
     A. zoos   **C.** rolling hills
     B. other areas   **D.** cages

_____ **10.** The new laws
     A. helped hunters   **C.** were not passed
     B. did not work   **D.** saved the turkeys

Shivering Is Not Just Quivering

Have you ever shivered on a cold day? You may not have noticed, but as you shivered, your body warmed up. Shivering is one way your body stays warm. It happens when signals are sent from the nervous system to the muscles. This is how it works.

The nervous system has two parts. One part is the nerves. They look like long, thin threads. Their job is to carry messages to all parts of the body. The spinal cord and the brain make up the other part of the nervous system. The spinal cord is a large bundle of nerves inside the backbone. Signals from the brain travel down the spinal cord. They go to the rest of the body through the nerves. Muscles receive these signals.

_____ **1.** Shivering helps your body

    A. keep calm   **C.** cool down

    B. stay warm   **D.** stand up straight

_____ **2.** Signals go from the nervous system to

    A. the muscles   **C.** the legs

    B. a certain cell   **D.** the nerves

_____ **3.** The nervous system has

    A. one part   **C.** two parts

    B. three parts   **D.** many parts

_____ **4.** Nerves look like

    A. muscles   **C.** blood cells

    B. threads   **D.** small trees

_____ **5.** The spinal cord is a large bundle of

    A. muscles   **C.** nerves

    B. brain cells   **D.** signals

Imagine waiting for a bus on a street corner. It's a cold day, the bus is late, and you feel chilled. Here's what happens.

A control center in your brain senses that you're cold. It sends a message down the spinal cord to all the nerves. The message races through nerves that connect to other nerves. Then it goes from the nerves to the muscles. The message says, "Warning! Prepare for action!"

When a muscle moves, it makes heat. That is why you get warm when you run or play soccer. When your muscles get the signal that you are cold, they get busy. First they become tight, then they loosen. They tighten then loosen over and over again. This makes you shiver. You also get warmer.

_____ **6.** Your brain's signal travels first to the
    A. bus   **C.** heart
    B. spinal cord   **D.** muscles

_____ **7.** Nerves tell the muscles to
    A. stop   **C.** get ready
    B. relax   **D.** cool down

_____ **8.** When a muscle moves, it becomes
    A. warm   **C.** stiff
    B. cool   **D.** heavy

_____ **9.** When you become cold, your muscles
    A. relax   **C.** stop moving
    B. stretch   **D.** tighten and loosen

_____ **10.** When you shiver, you get
    A. weaker   **C.** stronger
    B. colder   **D.** warmer

Good Night, Don't Bite!

There's nothing quite like falling sound asleep after a full day of work. Like people, animals need to rest after working hard. Some animals sleep floating in water. Others dig holes under the ground. Some even sleep high in trees or under leaves. But they all find a way to rest.

Animals sleeping in the sea can be a strange sight. Fish sleep with their eyes open. They do not have eyelids, so they seem to stare into the depths while they nap. Sea otters sometimes sleep in beds of seaweed. This keeps them from floating away. Parrotfish blow a clear gel from their mouths when they are ready to snooze. The gel forms a bubble around them. The bubble protects them from harm while they sleep.

_____ **1.** Like people, animals need to
    A. cry   **C.** rest
    B. talk   **D.** tell time

_____ **2.** Fish do not have
    A. scales   **C.** tails
    B. bubbles   **D.** eyelids

_____ **3.** Sea otters sometimes sleep in
    A. holes   **C.** boats
    B. seaweed   **D.** caves

_____ **4.** Parrotfish make a clear gel with their
    A. mouths   **C.** skin
    B. scales   **D.** fins

_____ **5.** Parrotfish sleep in a bubble that
    A. shrinks   **C.** grows large
    B. glows   **D.** protects them

Other animals sleep under the ground. Chipmunks sleep curled up in a ball. Their beds are made of leaves and grass. They wake up now and then to snack on food stored nearby. Some desert frogs dig underground holes during the hot, dry season. A frog may stay in its hole for months.

High above the ground, monkeys make leafy nests in trees each evening before they retire. The tree's high branches help to keep the monkeys safe during the night. Even the insects buzzing around their heads rest. Some sleep under a leaf that will be their next meal. A bee may crawl down into a blossom to rest. When it crawls out the next morning, it is rested and ready to buzz off to work.

_____ **6.** Chipmunks sleep in beds made of
    A. nets   **C.** leaves and grass
    B. mud   **D.** sticks and twigs

_____ **7.** Desert frogs stay underground during
    A. morning   **C.** the night
    B. winter   **D.** the hot, dry season

_____ **8.** Monkeys make beds using material from
    A. insects   **C.** the ground
    B. water   **D.** trees

_____ **9.** Some insects rest
    A. while eating   **C.** while buzzing
    B. under leaves   **D.** curled up in a ball

_____**10.** A bee might sleep in
    A. a flower   **C.** a bubble
    B. mud   **D.** clear gel

Stop That Pacing, Fido!

If you are planning a picnic, watch your pets. If your dog paces and your cat twitches, make other plans. It may rain that day. If you want to wash your car, go outside early in the day and look for a spider. If you see a spider spinning a web, get out your soap and bucket. There will most likely be fair weather.

If you would rather fly a kite, look at the stars the night before. If they are bright, find your kite and string. It will be windy the next day. But if you are more in the mood for a swim, listen to the crickets. By counting their chirps, you can tell if it is warm enough.

_____ **1.** If your cat twitches as you plan a picnic,
    A. wash your car   **C.** take more food
    B. go swimming   **D.** make other plans

_____ **2.** A spider spinning a web means
    A. rain   **C.** fair weather
    B. clouds   **D.** snow

_____ **3.** If you want to fly a kite, look at the
    A. dust   **C.** grass
    B. crickets   **D.** stars

_____ **4.** If you want to swim, listen to the
    A. crickets   **C.** cats
    B. dogs   **D.** spiders

_____ **5.** To tell about weather, count a cricket's
    A. legs   **C.** eyes
    B. chirps   **D.** wings

What do animals know about weather? Dampness collects in the air before rain. It makes each hair in an animal's fur swell. That is why your pets move about restlessly. Spiders do not like dampness in the air, either. A spiderweb will not stick to a damp surface. So if a spider is spinning a web, the air must be dry.

How can stars help you plan your fun? Stars are most easily seen when winds high in the air blow dust and clouds away. These winds will drop to the ground the next day, making it windy. What about those crickets? Count the number of times a cricket chirps in 15 seconds. Then add 37 to find out how warm it is. If you hear 35 chirps, it is 72 degrees.

_____ **6.** Dampness in the air makes an animal

    A. hungry   **C.** restless

    B. warm   **D.** smaller

_____ **7.** If a spider is spinning a web, the air must be

    A. damp   **C.** dry

    B. fresh   **D.** hot

_____ **8.** Strong winds high in the air blow away

    A. fur   **C.** stars

    B. webs   **D.** clouds

_____ **9.** If you see bright stars, there will be wind

    A. in a month   **C.** the following day

    B. in a week   **D.** in two days

_____ **10.** A cricket's chirps can help tell if it's

    A. warm   **C.** cloudy

    B. rainy   **D.** dusk

Louis Braille

Louis Braille was born in a small French town. When he was three, he lost his sight. At ten he went to a school for children who were blind. The books at his school were written with raised letters. He moved his fingers over the letters to read the books. Letters like *A* and *H* felt the same. He had a hard time understanding what he read.

Then Louis learned of a different way to read. It was used by soldiers who had to read messages in the dark. To write the messages, people punched dots in paper. Since the dots were raised, people could feel them.

_____ **1.** Louis Braille was born in
  A. Spain   **C.** England
  B. France   **D.** the United States

_____ **2.** Louis lost his sight when he was
  A. two   **C.** ten
  B. three   **D.** fifteen

_____ **3.** To read books Louis used
  A. his fingers **C.** a machine
  B. his eyes   **D.** his mother's help

_____ **4.** Louis had a hard time understanding
  A. his friends **C.** what he heard
  B. his teachers **D.** what he read

_____ **5.** The system with raised dots was used by
  A. miners   **C.** doctors
  B. soldiers   **D.** forest rangers

Louis liked the idea of reading with raised dots, but he thought it could be made simpler. So when Louis was fifteen, he made up a new way of writing. He used raised dots, but he made up his own alphabet.

All of Louis's friends at school liked his idea, but many teachers did not want to use it. They thought the old way worked just fine. Then in 1844, this new way of reading and writing was shown to the public. When more people saw how it worked, they liked it. Today people all over the world read books written in Braille.

_____ **6.** Louis decided to use the idea of reading
        A. old books   **C.** raised dots
        B. aloud   **D.** picture books

_____ **7.** Louis's new system used
        A. small letters   **C.** no raised dots
        B. a machine   **D.** a new alphabet

_____ **8.** Louis's friends thought his system
        A. was strange   **C.** worked well
        B. was too hard   **D.** did not work

_____ **9.** At first the new system was not used by
        A. parents   **C.** the government
        B. students   **D.** people who taught school

_____ **10.** Today Braille's system
        A. is not used   **C.** does not work
        B. is well liked   **D.** is used only in France

Writing Roundup

Read the story below. Think about the facts. Then answer the questions in complete sentences.

Have you ever seen a comet? It looks like a fuzzy star with a tail. It travels along a path in the sky. When the comet comes near the Sun, its tail looks long and bright.

Long ago most people thought that comets appeared by chance. They did not think comets traveled on a set path or time. But Edmond Halley disagreed. He was an English scientist. He claimed that comets came near the Sun at set times. Halley mapped the path of one comet. He had seen it in 1682. He predicted it would appear again in 1758. He was right. Today that comet is known as Halley's Comet. It is seen about every 77 years.

1. What does a comet look like?

_____

_____

2. When does a comet's tail look long and bright?

_____

_____

3. How often can Halley's Comet be seen?

_____

_____

Prewriting

Think of an idea you might write about, such as a planet or a way to travel in space. Write the idea in the center of the idea web below. Then fill out the rest of the web with facts.

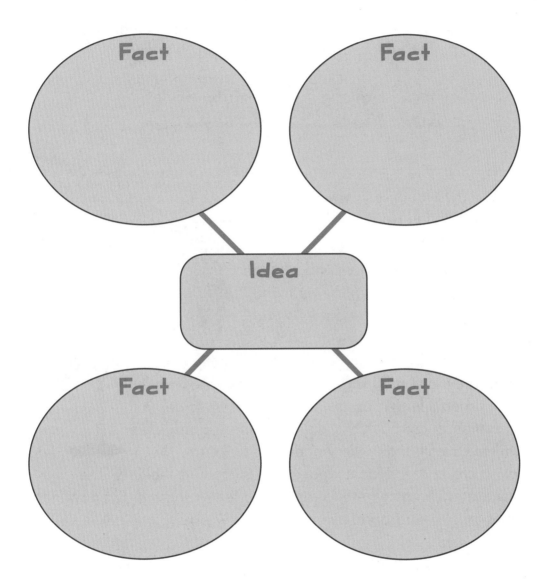

On Your Own

Now use another sheet of paper to write a story about your idea. Use the facts from your idea web.

What Is Sequence?

Sequence means time order. Events in a story happen in a sequence. Something happens first. Then other things happen.

How can you find the sequence in a story? Look for time words, such as *first*, *next*, and *last*. Here is a list of time words:

later	during	days of the week
today	while	months of the year

Try It!

Follow the sequence in this story. Circle all the time words.

Long ago a woodcutter and his wife lived in the forest. One day he found a lovely white crane caught in a trap. He freed the crane and went back to work. That night a young girl knocked on the couple's door. They took her inside. The next day she gave them a beautiful woven cloth and told them to sell it for a high price. Each day she gave them a new cloth. On the seventh night, the woodcutter woke up. He saw a crane at the loom weaving cloth from its feathers. The crane said, "I came here to repay you for saving me. But now I must go." It said good-bye and then flew away.

Try putting these events in the order that they happened. What happened first? Write the number **1** on the line by that sentence. Then write the number **2** by the sentence that tells what happened next. Write the number **3** by the sentence that tells what happened last.

_____ A young girl knocked on the couple's door.

_____ The woodcutter freed the crane from a trap.

_____ The girl gave the couple beautiful cloth.

Practice with Sequence

Here are some practice sequence questions. The first two are already answered. You can do the third one on your own.

___C___ **1.** When did the woodcutter see the crane at the loom?
    A. that evening
    B. at noon on the second day
    C. on the seventh night

Look at the question. Find the words *at the loom* in the story. They are in the sentence "He saw a crane at the loom weaving cloth from its feathers." The sentence before this one will tell you when he saw the crane. It says, "On the seventh night, the woodcutter woke up." So **C** is the correct answer. The man saw the crane at the loom on the seventh night.

___B___ **2.** What happened just before the crane flew away?
    A. The crane gave a cry of pain.
    B. The crane said good-bye.
    C. The crane wove cloth from its feathers.

Look at the question carefully. Notice the time word *before*. Also notice the word *just*. The question asks what happened *just before* the crane flew away. The sentence "It said good-bye and then flew away" tells you. The last thing the crane did before flying away was to say good-bye. So **B** is the correct answer.

_____ **3.** When did the crane weave the cloth?
    A. during the night
    B. in the morning
    C. in the afternoon

Can you find the answer?

Read each story. After each story you will answer questions about the sequence of events in the story. Remember, sequence is the order of things.

Long-Lost Note

Have you ever sealed a note inside of a bottle and thrown it into the sea? Many people have done this. Some have done it for fun, and others have done it for more serious reasons.

In 1784, a young Japanese sailor threw a bottle with a message into the sea. The sailor had been on a treasure hunt in the Pacific Ocean. A storm had come up, and his small ship had been wrecked. He and the other crew members had landed on a tiny island.

At first the men were happy. They were safe from the rough waves and the terrible wind. They waited for the storm to end. Finally the Sun came out. The men looked around. A few palm trees lay on the ground. There was nothing to eat except for some tiny crabs. Even worse, there wasn't any water to drink.

Soon the sailor was afraid that he and his friends would never leave the island. They would never see their families again. "Still," thought the sailor, "I might be able to send them a message."

He found a bottle in the wrecked ship. He cut thin pieces of wood from one of the trees. These pieces of wood would serve as paper. Slowly the sailor carved the story about the wreck into the wood. Then he put the message in the bottle and sealed it well. He tossed the bottle as far as he could into the ocean.

The sailor and his friends never left the island, but the bottle did. It rode the ocean waves for many years. Then one day the bottle washed up on the shore. A man found it tangled in some seaweed. He was very surprised! The bottle had landed in the very same village that was the sailor's home. The year was now 1935. The sailor's message had floated at sea for 150 years!

1. Put these events in the order that they happened. What happened first? Write the number **1** on the line by that sentence. Then write the number **2** by the sentence that tells what happened next. Write the number **3** by the sentence that tells what happened last.

_____ A big storm came up.

_____ The sailors landed on an island.

_____ The sailors hunted for buried treasure.

_____ **2.** When was the ship wrecked?
   A. before 1784
   B. during 1784
   C. after 1784

_____ **3.** When did the sailors look for food?
   A. after the storm
   B. before they reached the shore
   C. before they sailed away

_____ **4.** When did the sailor write his message?
   A. while the storm was coming
   B. after he had cut some wood
   C. after 1935

_____ **5.** When was the bottle found in the sailor's village?
   A. right after the sailor threw it into the sea
   B. 15 years after the sailor threw it into the sea
   C. 150 years after the sailor threw it into the sea

Dogs That Guide

In 1918, a doctor and his pet dog walked with a soldier who was blind. They were outside a German hospital. The doctor had to go in the building for a short time. The soldier and dog waited outside. When the doctor came out, the soldier and dog weren't there.

The doctor looked all around. He found them on the other side of the hospital yard. The doctor saw that his pet had led the soldier there safely. He thought a trained dog might be able to do more, so he taught a dog to lead a person. It worked out well. The German government helped start a program to teach dogs to be guides.

Dorothy Eustis went to Germany to find out about the guide dog course. When she came back to the United States, she wrote about it for a magazine. Soon more people knew of the guide dogs.

The best dogs for the job are smart and fit. They behave well and make good choices. It takes more than two years to train a puppy to be a guide dog. When the dog is 14 months old, it learns many commands. It learns to know right and left. It learns to cross a busy street, or not to cross if that puts its owner in danger. A dog is trained for months. Then the owner and the dog meet, and they practice for four weeks.

The first U.S. school for guide dogs opened in 1929. Now there are many schools, and there are more than 6,000 people with guide dogs.

1. Put these events in the order that they happened. What happened first? Write the number **1** on the line by that sentence. Then write the number **2** by the sentence that tells what happened next. Write the number **3** by the sentence that tells what happened last.

_____ The doctor saw the soldier and dog on the other side of the yard.

_____ The doctor taught a dog to lead a person.

_____ The doctor couldn't find the soldier and dog.

_____ **2.** When did the doctor go in the building?
   A. after he walked with the soldier
   B. after he looked all around
   C. after he found his pet dog

_____ **3.** What did Eustis do after she returned from Germany?
   A. found out about a guide dog course
   B. trained a dog
   C. wrote about the guide dog course

_____ **4.** When did the German government start a program to teach dogs to be guides?
   A. after Eustis went to Germany
   B. after the United States opened a guide dog school
   C. after the doctor taught a dog to lead a person

_____ **5.** When was the first guide dog school started in the United States?
   A. 1981
   B. 1929
   C. 1918

Traveling the Western Trail

Long ago moving west was not easy. There were no trains to Oregon or Washington. There were no airplanes or cars. People had to ride in covered wagons. They left their old way of life behind.

First people sold their farms. They took only their tools, seeds, and clothes with them. A fine horse or nice clothes were often left behind. They said good-bye to their families and friends forever.

The people rode a boat down a river to Independence, Missouri. From all across the East, people came to this town because it was located at the edge of the plains. There they bought wagons and mules. Then they loaded these wagons with food and supplies.

The people with wagons waited until spring. They waited for the grass to grow. The green grass would feed the mules during the trip. Once the plains turned green, everyone began the trip west in their wagons.

After three days they had to cross a river. Since it was spring, the river ran high. People made their mules jump into the cold water. Sometimes a family's food fell into the water. Many times the mules fell and could not get up. Still people had to keep moving forward.

The trip had to be made in six months. If it lasted longer, people would be trapped in the mountains during the winter. If they were trapped, they would freeze to death. The trip west was 2,000 miles long. Yet most people walked beside their wagons all the way to their new homes.

1. Put these events in the order that they happened. What happened first? Write the number **1** on the line by that sentence. Then write the number **2** by the sentence that tells what happened next. Write the number **3** by the sentence that tells what happened last.

_____ People rode a boat to Independence, Missouri.

_____ People sold their farms.

_____ People had to cross a river.

_____ **2.** When did people buy mules?
      A. after they rode the boat
      B. before they sold their farms
      C. during the summer

_____ **3.** When did the wagons start the trip west?
      A. in the fall
      B. during the spring
      C. in the winter

_____ **4.** How long did the trip take?
      A. fifteen months
      B. six months
      C. twelve months

_____ **5.** When did families sometimes lose their food?
      A. during the boat trip
      B. before crossing the plains
      C. when crossing a river

The Space Shuttle

Space shuttles go back and forth between Earth and space. The first one flew on April 12, 1981. A space shuttle has four main parts. They are the orbiter, the fuel tank, and two rocket boosters.

The orbiter looks like an airplane. It carries the crew. A huge tank is attached to the orbiter. It holds fuel for the orbiter's engines. A rocket booster is on each side of the tank. These fire on liftoff. In two minutes, the rockets run out of fuel and fall off. Parachutes slow their drop to the sea. Then boats tow them to shore. Rockets can be used as many as 20 times. The big tank runs out of fuel in eight minutes. It falls and breaks apart over the sea. Now the orbiter enters its orbit.

There may be up to seven crew members on board the orbiter. They do tests. They might launch satellites. In 1999, a shuttle went up to fix the Hubble telescope. The Hubble is as big as a bus. The shuttle caught it. The telescope was held in the cargo bay. That's an open place like the back of a pickup truck. The crew worked out in space to make repairs. They wore space suits. They were attached to the shuttle by a long line. A robot arm put the Hubble back in orbit.

When it's time to come home, the orbiter's engines fire. This slows the shuttle, and it drops from orbit. Tiles protect the shuttle from heat caused by entering Earth's atmosphere. The shuttle then acts like an airplane. It glides to a landing on a runway.

1. Put these events in the order that they happened. What happened first? Write the number **1** on the line by that sentence. Then write the number **2** by the sentence that tells what happened next. Write the number **3** by the sentence that tells what happened last.

_____ The shuttle drops from orbit.

_____ The orbiter's engines fire.

_____ The shuttle glides to a landing.

_____ **2.** When do the rocket boosters fire?
    A. while the orbiter is circling Earth
    B. right before landing
    C. on liftoff

_____ **3.** When does the orbiter enter its orbit?
    A. after the big fuel tank falls to the sea
    B. when the parachutes open
    C. after a satellite is launched

_____ **4.** When was the telescope held in the cargo bay?
    A. before 1999
    B. after the shuttle caught it
    C. after a robot arm put it in orbit

_____ **5.** When do the orbiter's engines fire?
    A. when it's time to return to Earth
    B. before it reaches orbit
    C. when the crew works out in space

How a Grizzly Spends the Winter

Imagine that it is a fall day in the Northwest. You are following a female grizzly bear. She walks through the woods looking for mice, berries, fruit, ant eggs, and honey. When she comes to a stream, she stops and swipes at fish. She catches a trout with one paw and swallows it quickly.

For days she is constantly on the move, searching for food. She may put on as many as 4 inches of fat at this time. Something tells the bear to stock up. She knows winter is coming.

As the days grow colder, the big bear begins looking for something else. She must find a place for her winter den. She digs a tunnel into the dirt on the side of a mountain. The hole is just a little larger than she is. She lines the den with moss, grass, or tree branches.

As winter comes closer, the grizzly begins to move more slowly. She drags herself from place to place. She looks as if she is half asleep. Finally one day when the snow is swirling around her, the grizzly crawls into her den. The snow soon covers the entrance. A person could stand 5 feet away and not know that the grizzly is there.

Sometime during the winter, the bear gives birth to two cubs. The cubs are very small and helpless. The mother bear takes good care of them. She nurses them and keeps them warm. In the spring they are old enough to leave the den. She teaches them to hunt for food. The young cubs stay with their mother for a year and a half.

1. Put these events in the order that they happened. What happened first? Write the number **1** on the line by that sentence. Then write the number **2** by the sentence that tells what happened next. Write the number **3** by the sentence that tells what happened last.

_____ The mother grizzly teaches the cubs to hunt.

_____ The cubs leave their mother.

_____ The baby cubs are born.

_____ **2.** When do grizzlies eat constantly?
     A. after they have cubs
     B. during winter
     C. in the fall

_____ **3.** When do grizzlies look for a place to dig their winter dens?
     A. when the days get colder
     B. while they are helpless
     C. in the spring

_____ **4.** When do grizzlies crawl into their dens?
     A. when it is very humid
     B. when it begins snowing
     C. when it begins raining

_____ **5.** When do grizzlies give birth to their cubs?
     A. during the summer
     B. in the spring
     C. during the winter

Black Widow Spiders

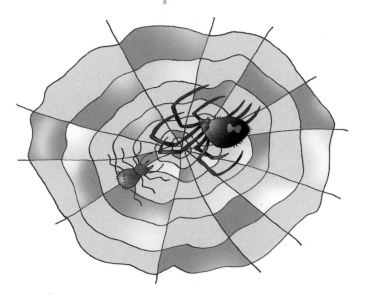

Did you know that the black widow spider is one of the most poisonous spiders in the world? But only the females can hurt you. The males are harmless. The female's poison is much stronger than that of a rattlesnake. A person who has been bitten can die if he or she does not get treatment.

The female black widow is about $\frac{1}{2}$ inch long. She is black and has red marks on her belly. The black widow gets her name from the fact that she sometimes eats her mate. The male is $\frac{1}{3}$ of the female's size. He doesn't have any red marks.

Let's observe one black widow female. When we first see her, she is hanging upside down in her web. She stays there for three days without moving. Her skin becomes too small, so she sheds it. She grows a new, larger skin. This is called molting, and it happens about eight times during her life.

One day a male black widow comes to the edge of the female's web. He strums on the web. If the female is ready to mate, she will strum also. If not, she may chase and eat him. It is unsafe to be a male black widow.

After mating, the female weaves a small silk sac. This is where she will lay from 250 to 750 eggs. Black widows lay their eggs in the spring. The female guards the egg sac for about a month. Then baby spiders, or spiderlings, hatch. The spiderlings are small and helpless when they come out of the egg sac. Many are eaten by birds or insects. Some are even eaten by their mother. Most, however, live and become adults.

1. Put these events in the order that they happened. What happened first? Write the number **1** on the line by that sentence. Then write the number **2** by the sentence that tells what happened next. Write the number **3** by the sentence that tells what happened last.

_____ The spiderlings hatch.

_____ The female makes the egg sac.

_____ The male black widow strums on the web.

_____ **2.** When does the female black widow hang in her web without moving?
     A. after eating
     B. before laying eggs
     C. while she is molting

_____ **3.** When does the female black widow strum on her web?
     A. when she is ready to mate
     B. when she is hungry
     C. when she is sleepy

_____ **4.** When does the female make an egg sac?
     A. when she is molting
     B. after mating
     C. before biting someone

_____ **5.** When do black widows lay their eggs?
     A. in the spring
     B. during summer
     C. before the first snow

Trains of the Past

In the early 1800s, horses pulled wagons over wooden rails. These were the first American trains. These trains could go only a short distance. Only a few cars could be pulled at once.

A big improvement was made in the 1830s. The first steam engines were used. They used wood as fuel to feed a fire. The fire burned and turned the water inside the engine into steam. The steam made pistons move back and forth. The pistons moved rods that turned the wheels. Wood was used for about the next 40 years.

After the Civil War, steam engines used coal instead of wood. Coal burned longer and made a better fuel. It was burned to heat water and make steam in the same way that wood was used.

From 1900 to 1935, the design of trains did not change much. Trains from these years are called the classic trains. Some people think these are the best trains ever made. Many passengers rode on trains at this time. A classic train had a dining car, a lounge, and Pullman cars. The seats in a Pullman car changed into beds. Passengers could get a good night's sleep on their long trips.

Trains used the steam engine for about 60 years. In the 1930s the diesel engine appeared. The classic trains were replaced by streamliner trains. Today you might ride on a double-deck superliner train.

1. Put these events in the order that they happened. What happened first? Write the number **1** on the line by that sentence. Then write the number **2** by the sentence that tells what happened next. Write the number **3** by the sentence that tells what happened last.

_____ The diesel engine appeared.

_____ Steam engines used wood as fuel.

_____ Steam engines used coal as fuel.

_____ **2.** When did horses pull trains?
  A. during the Revolutionary War
  B. in the early 1800s
  C. around 1935

_____ **3.** When were steam engines first used?
  A. from 1900 to 1935
  B. after the Civil War
  C. around 1830

_____ **4.** When did the classic trains run?
  A. when superliners appeared
  B. in the early 1800s
  C. from 1900 to 1935

_____ **5.** When did diesel engines appear?
  A. in the 1930s
  B. from 1900 to 1935
  C. before the Civil War

Animal Partners

What would you do if your back itched in a place you couldn't reach? What if you couldn't get a jar open? You would probably ask someone to help you. Did you know that animals also help each other? Sometimes they form strange partnerships.

Two animals in Africa are partners. They help each other get their favorite food. A small bird called the honey guide likes to eat beeswax. The bird has a good sense of smell. It can find a hive from far away. Its beak is not strong enough to break into the hive, so the honey guide flies off in search of its partner—the ratel.

The ratel is a mammal. It loves honey! It has sharp claws and a tough hide to keep it from getting stung. When the honey guide finds a ratel, it hops and chatters. The ratel follows the honey guide to the hive. The ratel breaks open the hive and eats the honey. Then the honey guide eats the wax and grubs inside. Both animals get what they want. The only loser is the bee!

The crocodile and crocodile bird are also good partners. The crocodile often gets food stuck between its teeth when it is eating. Leeches bite its tongue. When the crocodile bird is around, the crocodile opens its mouth. Sometimes it leaves its mouth open for hours. The bird hops into the crocodile's mouth. It eats the leeches and bits of food. The bird also eats ticks on the crocodile's back. In this partnership both animals gain something. The crocodile has its back and mouth cleaned. The crocodile bird has dinner.

1. Put these events in the order that they happened. What happened first? Write the number **1** on the line by that sentence. Then write the number **2** by the sentence that tells what happened next. Write the number **3** by the sentence that tells what happened last.

_____ The honey guide eats the beeswax.

_____ The honey guide smells a beehive.

_____ The honey guide searches for a ratel.

_____ **2.** When does a honey guide look for a ratel?
    A. when it needs protection
    B. before it makes its nest
    C. when it finds a beehive

_____ **3.** When does the honey guide eat the beeswax?
    A. after the ratel has broken the hive open
    B. before looking for the ratel
    C. when it first smells the hive

_____ **4.** When does the crocodile need to have its mouth cleaned?
    A. when it is hungry
    B. after it has eaten
    C. when it is sleeping

_____ **5.** When does the crocodile hold open its mouth?
    A. when it is tired
    B. when the crocodile bird is cleaning
    C. when it has ticks

Writing Roundup

Read the story below. Think about the sequence, or time order. Answer the questions in complete sentences.

During lunch, Leo said that he had a rock collection. Later Jonelle thought of what to get him for his birthday. She told Duane her idea. Duane told two more friends. At his party Leo first unwrapped Jonelle's gift. It was a piece of quartz. Next Duane gave him a piece of marble. After that he got flint and slate. Leo smiled and said thanks. He didn't tell his friends he collected rock music.

1. When did Leo say he had a rock collection?

_____

_____

2. After opening his rock gifts, what did Leo do?

_____

_____

3. When did Jonelle think of a gift for Leo?

_____

_____

4. When did Leo open Duane's present?

_____

_____

Prewriting

Think about something that you have done, such as wrapping a gift, playing baseball, or going through a cafeteria line. Write the events in sequence below.

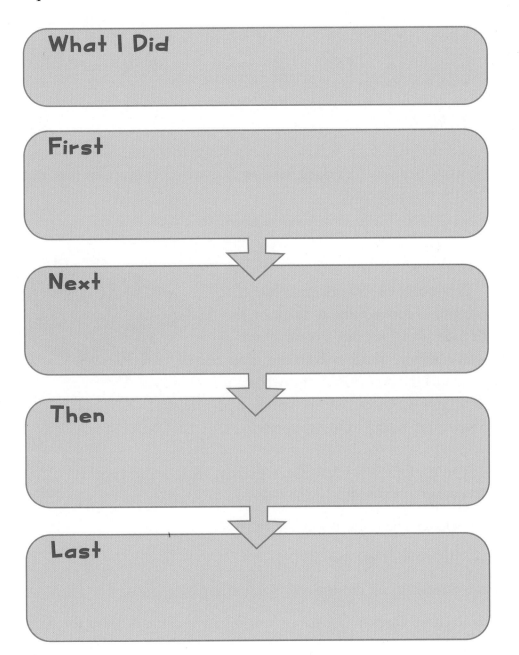

What I Did

First

Next

Then

Last

On Your Own

Now use another sheet of paper to write a story about what you have done. Write the events in the order that they happened. Use time order words.

What Is Context?

Context means all the words in a sentence or all the sentences in a paragraph. If you find a word you do not know, look at the words around it. These other words can help you figure out what the word means.

Try It!

Read the paragraph below. It has a word that you may not know. The word is printed in **dark letters**. See whether you can find out what the word means.

Sheena's best friend gave her a present. It looked like a book on the outside. But the pages were blank. It was a **diary**. Sheena liked the idea of making her own book. She writes in it every day. She writes about her family and friends. She writes about training her dog.

If you don't know what **diary** means, look at the context. This paragraph contains these words:

Clue: looked like a book on the outside

Clue: the pages were blank

Clue: Sheena liked the idea of making her own book.

Find these clues in the paragraph. Draw a circle around them. What words do you think of when you read the clues? Write the words below:

_____

Did you write *journal*? The context clue words tell you that a **diary** is a journal or record of what you do every day.

Working with Context

This unit asks questions that you can answer by using context clues in paragraphs. There are two kinds of paragraphs. The paragraphs in the first part of this book have blank spaces in them. You can use the context clues in the paragraphs to decide which word should go in each space. Here is an example:

> Animals have different kinds of feet. Squirrels have long toes with sharp ___1___ that help them climb trees. A mountain goat's ___2___ help it go up steep cliffs.

B **1.** **A.** fingers **B.** claws **C.** gloves **D.** knives

_____ **2.** **A.** hooves **B.** hands **C.** nails **D.** boots

Look at the answer choices for question 1. Treat the paragraph as a puzzle. Which pieces don't fit? Which piece fits best? Try putting each word in the blank. See which one makes the most sense. Squirrels don't have sharp *fingers* or *gloves* or *knives*. *Claws* (answer **B**) is the only choice that makes sense. Now try to answer question 2 on your own.

The paragraphs in the second part of this unit are different. For these you figure out the meaning of a word that is printed in **dark letters** in the paragraph. Here is an example:

> The Inuit people use **kayaks** to travel the icy waters where they live. Kayaks are like canoes, but they have room for only one person.

The word in dark type is **kayaks**. Find the context clues. Then choose a word that means the same as **kayaks**.

_____ **3.** In this paragraph, the word **kayaks** means
    A. sleds   **C.** boats
    B. skis   **D.** planes

Read the passages and answer the questions about context. Remember, context is a way to learn new words by thinking about the other words used in a story.

The California condor is dying out. Only 27 of these large birds were still living in 1987. Some people started raising condors in a zoo. They took eggs from condor nests. The eggs ___1___. Then the baby birds lived in the zoo. It took ___2___ years for the condors to grow up. Then they were turned loose.

_____ 1. A. sang   B. behaved   C. locked   D. hatched

_____ 2. A. several   B. bad   C. bent   D. deep

Some wasps build their nests out of paper. They chew wood. They ___3___ it with juice in their mouths. Then they ___4___ out the wet mixture and make their nests.

_____ 3. A. mix   B. paste   C. hurt   D. bake

_____ 4. A. kick   B. spit   C. shoot   D. hug

Magic Johnson was a basketball superstar. He practiced every day when he was a ___5___. He practiced bouncing the ball. He practiced ___6___ the ball. Magic said that it's hard to practice every day, but that's how to become a winner!

_____ 5. A. teacher   B. coach   C. batter   D. youth

_____ 6. A. sliding   B. hunting   C. shooting   D. sitting

Guide dogs are helpful to people who are blind. The dog wears a ___7___ with a long handle. The owner holds the handle. Then the person gives ___8___. The dog obeys them. It carefully guides its owner across streets.

_____ 7. A. coat   B. harness   C. shirt   D. belt

_____ 8. A. fences   B. jars   C. toys   D. commands

People in Russia give eggs as gifts. They do not give just plain white eggs. The eggs are painted with pictures. Many of the pictures have ___9___ meanings, such as "good luck" and "long life." In Russia, ___10___ eggs become little works of art!

_____ 9. **A.** special   **B.** cold   **C.** small   **D.** purple

_____10. **A.** lizard   **B.** ordinary   **C.** red   **D.** broken

---

A man wondered whether bees know which flowers to go to. So he drew flowers on a large ___11___ of paper. Half the flowers were blue. The other half were yellow. On each blue flower, he put a big cup of sugar water. He put a ___12___ cup on each yellow flower. The bees stopped going to the yellow flowers.

_____11. **A.** test   **B.** row   **C.** sheet   **D.** pencil

_____12. **A.** big   **B.** tiny   **C.** glass   **D.** slow

---

Some plants don't have seeds. How can you grow a seedless grape plant? First cut off a piece of ___13___ from a grape plant. Put it in water. Soon it begins to grow roots. Plant it in the ___14___ . It will grow into a new grape plant.

_____13. **A.** stem   **B.** tree   **C.** spoon   **D.** stone

_____14. **A.** step   **B.** dirt   **C.** green   **D.** road

---

Sounds can move through air or water. Sounds bounce back if they hit a ___15___ object. Then you can hear them a second time. These ___16___ sounds are called echoes.

_____15. **A.** solid   **B.** mean   **C.** burned   **D.** eager

_____16. **A.** fair   **B.** forty   **C.** pink   **D.** repeated

Animals have different ways to escape from ___1___. Some run very fast. Others climb trees. Some are safe because they are hard to see. They may be the same color as the ground. They may look like plants. They may have ___2___ or spots that look like the shadows of trees. Instead of running, these animals stand very still.

_____ 1. **A.** mice   **B.** danger   **C.** clouds   **D.** help

_____ 2. **A.** stripes   **B.** teeth   **C.** string   **D.** soup

Every year in Thailand, people have Elephant Day. They bring their elephants to one ___3___. Everyone comes to see whose elephant is the best. The elephants run a race. They also carry big logs and ___4___ them in a pile.

_____ 3. **A.** bit   **B.** fault   **C.** location   **D.** paper

_____ 4. **A.** think   **B.** climb   **C.** stack   **D.** sneeze

Have you ever ___5___ a pill bug? These animals are not pills or bugs! They got the name *pill* because they can roll up into a ball. They got the name *bug* because of their small ___6___. Pill bugs belong to the same family as crabs.

_____ 5. **A.** counted   **B.** run   **C.** cried   **D.** observed

_____ 6. **A.** answers   **B.** size   **C.** day   **D.** park

A giant toad finds ___7___ in a cool, damp place. At night the toad comes out. It needs food for its huge ___8___. The toad eats as many insects as it can find.

_____ 7. **A.** cows   **B.** magic   **C.** money   **D.** shelter

_____ 8. **A.** leg   **B.** appetite   **C.** suit   **D.** rule

A man used an airplane to cover his gas ___9___. He hoped people would then stop to buy gas. He bought a B-17 airplane. It took three big machines to ___10___ the plane onto poles. Then he put lights under the wings. People could look up at the plane while they filled their cars up with gas.

_____ 9. **A.** well   **B.** hole   **C.** tank   **D.** station

_____ 10. **A.** fly   **B.** elevate   **C.** begin   **D.** drive

Turtles ___11___ to be very slow animals. Many turtles are really very ___12___ . Sea turtles can swim quickly. The green turtle can swim as fast as 20 miles per hour for a short time.

_____ 11. **A.** appear   **B.** alarm   **C.** nibble   **D.** hide

_____ 12. **A.** young   **B.** huge   **C.** plain   **D.** speedy

The moray eel lives in warm ocean waters. It is a strong fish with very sharp teeth. The eel hides in a hole or cave. It can catch fish with ___13___ speed. The moray eel will not ___14___ out from its hole to look for food until it is night.

_____ 13. **A.** brave   **B.** dry   **C.** lightning   **D.** half

_____ 14. **A.** blink   **B.** venture   **C.** list   **D.** roll

Some people think Lincoln wrote the Gettysburg Address on a ___15___ of paper. This is ___16___ . He wrote it carefully on a whole sheet of paper. He changed the words four times. Every time he changed the words, he copied it over again.

_____ 15. **A.** letter   **B.** scrap
             C. ship   **D.** chain

_____ 16. **A.** incorrect   **B.** sad
             C. large   **D.** useful

Totem poles are tall wooden poles with animals painted on them. The animals look __1__. Parts of them look like people. One part of each animal sticks out. Bears have huge claws. Beavers have long front teeth. Crows have long, straight __2__.

_____ 1. **A.** better   **B.** unreal   **C.** orange   **D.** unhappy

_____ 2. **A.** noses   **B.** arms   **C.** buttons   **D.** beaks

The first Ferris wheel was taller than a building 20 stories high. George Ferris made the giant wheel ride for the 1893 World's Fair. It had 36 cars. It held many __3__. At the top of the wheel, everyone could see for __4__.

_____ 3. **A.** passengers   **B.** puppets   **C.** rulers   **D.** balls

_____ 4. **A.** glasses   **B.** animals   **C.** miles   **D.** hours

The numbat has sharp claws on its front feet. The numbat uses these to tear open __5__ logs. Then it puts its long, sticky __6__ inside to catch termites. A numbat eats only termites.

_____ 5. **A.** yellow   **B.** square   **C.** red   **D.** rotten

_____ 6. **A.** brain   **B.** tongue   **C.** fin   **D.** eye

There is gold in ocean water. The __7__ is getting it out. Since the gold there is __8__, taking it out of the ocean costs a lot of money. Maybe one day someone will find an easy way to do it.

_____ 7. **A.** bank   **B.** team   **C.** number   **D.** problem

_____ 8. **A.** scarce   **B.** light   **C.** free   **D.** nickel

Harriet Tubman was a slave who escaped to __9__ in the North. She worried about the slaves still in the South, so she returned many times. Each time, she helped slaves escape. A huge __10__ was offered to anyone who caught her. No one ever did.

_____ 9. **A.** nowhere   **B.** rains   **C.** us   **D.** freedom

_____ 10. **A.** reward   **B.** trunk   **C.** cave   **D.** seal

In the spring some fish leave the __11__ where they live. They swim __12__ in rivers to ponds where they were born. These fish can find their way even when their eyes are covered. They get lost if their noses are covered. The fish use their noses to find their way!

_____ 11. **A.** ocean   **B.** valley   **C.** basket   **D.** leaf

_____ 12. **A.** everywhere   **B.** hardly   **C.** upstream   **D.** here

Smog is usually a mix of smoke and fog. It can also come from the sun acting on __13__ in the air. Smog can __14__ a person's health and kill plant life. Smog can be very thick, making it hard to see things.

_____ 13. **A.** stars   **B.** fumes   **C.** pals   **D.** pens

_____ 14. **A.** fix   **B.** save   **C.** give   **D.** damage

Puffins are birds that live on northern coasts. __15__ of puffins stay at sea most of the time. They swim and dive to catch fish. They come on land to nest on high __16__.

_____ 15. **A.** Pans   **B.** Friends   **C.** Flocks   **D.** Barns

_____ 16. **A.** cliffs   **B.** seas   **C.** nets   **D.** pits

Peanut butter was first made by George Washington Carver. He also ____1____ many other ways to use peanuts. Carver wanted to help farmers. He hoped they could make money raising peanuts. His wish came true. Farmers started making money. Kids started ____2____ peanut butter!

_____ **1.** **A.** carried   **B.** discovered   **C.** filled   **D.** raked

_____ **2.** **A.** enjoying   **B.** losing   **C.** wearing   **D.** drinking

In Florida it's too warm for snow. One year people there had a Snow Day. They got a snow machine. The machine made a snow pile that was two ____3____ high. The people had so much fun they ____4____ to have a Snow Day every year.

_____ **3.** **A.** plants   **B.** heads   **C.** books   **D.** stories

_____ **4.** **A.** decided   **B.** believed   **C.** blinked   **D.** drove

Dark ____5____ on the Sun are called sunspots. They look dark because they are cooler than the rest of the Sun. Large spots may take weeks to fade away, while small ones ____6____ in just hours.

_____ **5.** **A.** patches   **B.** dust   **C.** kits   **D.** leaves

_____ **6.** **A.** remember   **B.** swim   **C.** vanish   **D.** use

Water lilies grow year after year. Their roots ____7____ to the bottom of a lake or stream. Their large leaves float. Strong stems hold the flowers above water. Some water lilies bloom during the day. Others bloom ____8____ at night.

_____ **7.** **A.** see   **B.** cling   **C.** thaw   **D.** pierce

_____ **8.** **A.** loudly   **B.** solely   **C.** wisely   **D.** barely

You may think of beavers as the ___9___ of the animal world. Beavers have strong front teeth. They cut down many trees. They use the branches to build ___10___ for homes in the water. Beavers use the bark for food.

_____ 9. **A.** keepers   **B.** lumberjacks   **C.** pilots   **D.** knights

_____ 10. **A.** lodges   **B.** pillows   **C.** motors   **D.** porches

---

The elf owl is most often found in dry areas of the country. It sits still in its nest during the day. Then the owl flies out to feed at ___11___. It uses its ___12___ senses to find food.

_____ 11. **A.** market   **B.** sundown   **C.** breakfast   **D.** feather

_____ 12. **A.** flat   **B.** outside   **C.** fat   **D.** keen

---

BOLD is a group that helps people who are blind learn to ski. The helpers tell how the ski trail looks. They follow the skiers. They say when to turn. They teach other skiing ___13___. The blind people ski on the same trails as ___14___ else.

_____ 13. **A.** skills   **B.** fiddles   **C.** hairs   **D.** stairs

_____ 14. **A.** all   **B.** somebody   **C.** everyone   **D.** someone

---

The king or queen of England owns the crown jewels. These ___15___ include crowns, rings, bracelets, ___16___, and swords. They are kept safe in the Tower of London.

_____ 15. **A.** treasures   **B.** monkeys
              C. carts   **D.** trails

_____ 16. **A.** tribes   **B.** doors
              C. thoughts   **D.** necklaces

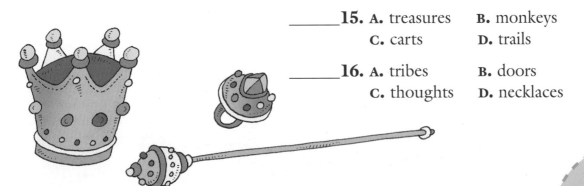

Larry Nyce builds tiny railroads. He makes the trains himself instead of **purchasing** them from a store. He lays the tracks on tiny wooden railroad ties. He makes tiny trees from sticks and little mountains from rocks.

_____ **1.** In this paragraph, the word **purchasing** means
    A. selling   **C.** buying
    B. riding   **D.** carrying

One kind of lizard changes colors to match the thing it is standing on. These lizards can be green like leaves. They can be brown like tree bark. If you put one on an apple, the lizard will not turn **scarlet**. It can match only the colors in its outdoor home.

_____ **2.** In this paragraph, the word **scarlet** means
    A. shiny   **C.** red
    B. spotted   **D.** juicy

The Inca people lived 500 years ago. Today some people remember the old Incan ways by dressing in Incan **costumes**. They wear hats with feathers on top and gold chains hanging down.

_____ **3.** In this paragraph, the word **costumes** means
    A. clothes   **C.** kings
    B. parades   **D.** faces

The polar bear is a large bear with white fur. The polar bear's color helps it. The white fur blends with the white snow. The bear can **sneak** up on a seal without being seen.

_____ **4.** In this paragraph, the word **sneak** means
    A. spill   **C.** arrange
    B. creep   **D.** hang

Running is fun. Some people like to run against each other. Most people **prefer** to run against themselves. They may try to run more and more miles each day, or they may try to run for longer and longer times.

_____ **5.** In this paragraph, the word **prefer** means

    A. help   **C.** measure

    B. shop   **D.** like

Many animals live in shell houses, but they get their shells in different ways. A turtle's shell is really part of its skeleton. It wears its bones on the outside. A **clam** has no bones. It makes its shell from salt in the ocean.

_____ **6.** In this paragraph, the word **clam** means

    A. shark   **C.** small land animal

    B. fish   **D.** kind of sea animal

Babe Ruth was the home-run king for a long time. He hit a record 714 home runs. Ruth played his last game in 1935. Then he **retired**. It took almost 40 years for someone to break his record.

_____ **7.** In this paragraph, the word **retired** means

    A. quit work   **C.** went to sleep

    B. played songs **D.** forgot something

There are giant ships more than 700 feet long. These ships were built to carry tons of wheat from place to place. They have a road folded up in back. When they get to shore, the road unfolds. The **cargo** is moved on and off.

_____ **8.** In this paragraph, the word **cargo** means

    A. truck   **C.** load

    B. garbage   **D.** flower

Sherlock Holmes is a great detective, but he lives only in books. The **tales** about him have been written in 57 languages.

_____ **1.** In this paragraph, the word **tales** means
    A. places   **C.** stories
    B. names   **D.** pens

The most important part of a running shoe is the part under your foot. This bottom part must be thick and soft. That is so it will **cushion** your foot as you run. A good shoe can keep you running well for a long time.

_____ **2.** In this paragraph, the word **cushion** means
    A. bring   **C.** protect
    B. tie   **D.** enter

Birds **perch** on a tree even while they sleep. Their toes grab the branch so they don't fall. Three toes point forward. One toe points backward. The toes lock tightly onto the branch.

_____ **3.** In this paragraph, the word **perch** means
    A. fly   **C.** vanish
    B. sit   **D.** promise

Doctors studied thousands of people. Some of the people spent most of their time alone. Many of these people had weak hearts. They were more likely to have a heart attack. Other people spent much time with their families and friends. Most of these **social** people had strong hearts.

_____ **4.** In this paragraph, the word **social** means
    A. lonely   **C.** strange
    B. friendly   **D.** sick

Car builders might make a new kind of car. The car will have a kind of **vision**. It will warn you if something is in your way. The car will be able to see a small child. It will be able to see a wall that is too close when you are parking.

_____ **5.** In this paragraph, the word **vision** means
- **A.** smell
- **B.** light
- **C.** sight
- **D.** window

Sugar **arrived** in Europe hundreds of years ago. Traders brought it from the East. At first people used sugar as medicine. It was many years before people used sugar to make desserts.

_____ **6.** In this paragraph, the word **arrived** means
- **A.** read
- **B.** appeared
- **C.** nodded
- **D.** tested

Tears are good for your eyes. They wash away dirt and help keep germs out of your eyes. Tears **bathe** your eyes all the time to keep them from getting too dry.

_____ **7.** In this paragraph, the word **bathe** means
- **A.** wash
- **B.** dry
- **C.** kiss
- **D.** lift

The armadillo can swim across a river. It **gulps** air into its stomach to make it float. Then it just paddles toward the other side!

_____ **8.** In this paragraph, the word **gulps** means
- **A.** heats
- **B.** plows
- **C.** shakes
- **D.** swallows

Ferns are plants without flowers. Most ferns live in **mild** climates, but some ferns can grow in cold places.

_____ **1.** In this paragraph, the word **mild** means

A. warm **C.** noisy

B. cheerful **D.** sour

A man wanted to be the first to see a desert that had never been explored. He bought two camels and set out. The trip took 19 days. He got lost and ran out of water. He was **exhausted** from walking in the heat. He lost 60 pounds, but he finally made it!

_____ **2.** In this paragraph, the word **exhausted** means

A. very shy **C.** very afraid

B. very tired **D.** very ready

Some jungle animals travel by air. They may look as if they are flying, but they're not. They're gliding. They leap from a high branch and **descend** to a lower branch.

_____ **3.** In this paragraph, the word **descend** means

A. go down **C.** jump up

B. fly by **D.** cross over

The tiger cat lives in Australia. It runs fast and also climbs trees well. The tiger cat looks for small animals at night. This cat hunts **restlessly** until it catches its dinner.

_____ **4.** In this paragraph, the word **restlessly** means

A. in cities **C.** while sleeping

B. under water **D.** without stopping

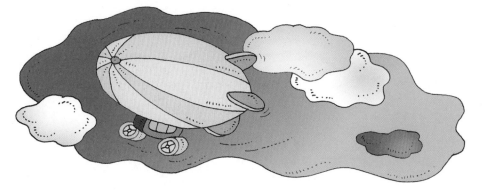

A blimp is a small airship. It doesn't have a metal frame to give it shape. But a blimp does have a strong bag that is filled with gas. The gas makes the blimp float. When the gas is taken out, the blimp **collapses**.

_____ **5.** In this paragraph, the word **collapses** means

    A. falls down   **C.** flies off

    B. works out   **D.** takes over

Trees are important. Their roots help hold soil in place and keep it from being washed away by rains. Tree roots also help hold **moisture** in the ground and keep it from drying out.

_____ **6.** In this paragraph, the word **moisture** means

    A. cloth   **C.** dampness

    B. morning   **D.** safety

There is a huge copper mine in Utah. The mine is an open pit. It is about 1/2 mile deep and more than 2 miles wide at the top. This mine has **yielded** more copper than any other mine.

_____ **7.** In this paragraph, the word **yielded** means

    A. bowed   **C.** stretched

    B. supplied   **D.** divided

Baby geese are called goslings. The mother goose does not have to teach them how to behave like geese. The goslings can swim and dive without **instruction**.

_____ **8.** In this paragraph, the word **instruction** means

    A. frogs   **C.** crowns

    B. books   **D.** lessons

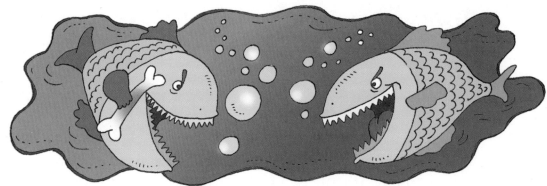

Piranhas are fish. They live in South American rivers. These fish tend to swim in large groups. They will tear the flesh off an animal or person that gets in the water. In just minutes all that is left is the **skeleton**.

_____ **1.** In this paragraph, the word **skeleton** means

    A. key   **C.** butter

    B. pie   **D.** bones

A cartoon is a **humorous** way to tell a story or make a point. A cartoon can be one drawing or a set of drawings. A cartoon may have words with the picture, but words aren't always needed.

_____ **2.** In this paragraph, the word **humorous** means

    A. cozy   **C.** dangerous

    B. funny   **D.** thirsty

Usually Pluto is the planet farthest from the Sun. Not much is known about this **distant** planet. It is quite cold there since it is so far from the Sun. Scientists don't think that there is any life on Pluto.

_____ **3.** In this paragraph, the word **distant** means

    A. faraway   **C.** lucky

    B. nearby   **D.** pleasant

Long ago, **vessels** crossed the water from northern Europe to other countries. They carried Viking warriors. At first the Vikings fought with people. Then the Vikings decided to trade. They set up many new trade centers.

_____ **4.** In this paragraph, the word **vessels** means

    A. whales   **C.** ships

    B. bottles   **D.** horses

The bluebonnet is one flower that really helps bees. A bluebonnet has a white spot on it. After a bee has visited this flower and taken nectar, the white spot turns red. The other bees don't waste time. They know they will be **disappointed** if they go to the blue flowers with red spots.

_____ **5.** In this paragraph, the word **disappointed** means

    A. pretty   **C.** large

    B. hot   **D.** sorry

The Negev Desert covers half of Israel. The soil in this desert is **fertile**. People can grow crops there. They use water from a nearby sea. Special hoses spray water on the crops.

_____ **6.** In this paragraph, the word **fertile** means

    A. rich   **C.** greedy

    B. glad   **D.** sharp

The Aztecs lived long ago. They were a great tribe. They built a **glorious** city. Now this city is known as Mexico City.

_____ **7.** In this paragraph, the word **glorious** means

    A. foolish   **C.** corner

    B. grand   **D.** helpless

Plants can be grown without soil. They grow in special water. The water has everything that plants need to grow. This **style** of farming is called hydroponics. It can be used in space.

_____ **8.** In this paragraph, the word **style** means

    A. center   **C.** rush

    B. garden   **D.** type

Writing Roundup

Read each paragraph. Write a word that makes sense on each line.

Sara got out the water hose and bucket and gave her dog Dusty a bath. Dusty did not like to be

(1) _____. As soon as his bath was over,

he rolled in the (2) _____.

Our family likes to go camping. It's fun to sit outside the tent at night and look up at the (3) _____. I wish we could go camping every

(4) _____.

A new boy came to our

(5) _____ today. We

wanted to be friendly, so we asked

him to (6) _____

with us.

Read each paragraph. Complete each sentence with a word or words that make sense in the paragraph.

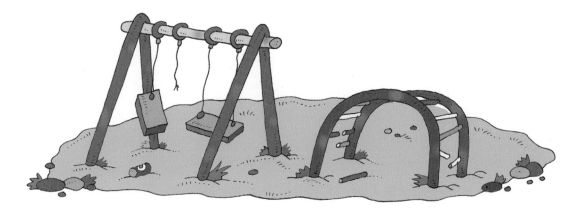

One corner of the school playground did not look pretty. Mr. Jackson's class wanted to make it look better. At first they thought about

(1) _____.

Then they talked to **(2)** _____

_____.

Now they knew they would **(3)** _____

_____.

Jamal went shopping for a gift for his mother. First he went to **(4)** _____

_____.

Nothing that he found seemed just right. Then he saw **(5)** _____.

"I know!" he cried. "I'll get her **(6)** _____

_____!"

What Is a Main Idea?

The main idea of a story tells what it is about. The other sentences add details to the main idea. Often the main idea is stated in the first or last sentence of the paragraph. Sometimes you may find the main idea in the middle of the paragraph.

This example may help you think about main ideas:

5	+	6	+	7	=	18
detail	+	detail	+	detail	=	main idea

The *5*, *6*, and *7* are like details. They are smaller than their sum, *18*. The *18*, like a main idea, is bigger. It is made of several smaller parts.

Try It!

Read the story below. Draw a line under the main idea.

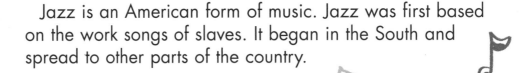

Jazz is an American form of music. Jazz was first based on the work songs of slaves. It began in the South and spread to other parts of the country.

The main idea sentence is the first sentence in the story. All the other sentences are details. They give more facts about jazz.

The main idea could come at the end of the story:

Jazz was first based on the work songs of slaves. It began in the South and spread to other parts of the country. Jazz is an American form of music.

Practice Finding the Main Idea

This unit asks you to find main ideas. Read the story and answer the question below.

There are more than 3,000 kinds of frogs. The grass frog is so small it can sit on an acorn. The goliath frog of West Africa is the largest frog in the world. It is the size of a cat. The water-holding frog uses the skin it has shed to make a bag around itself. This bag holds in water and keeps the frog cool.

___C___ 1. The story mainly tells
- **A.** about the goliath frog
- **B.** about a tiny frog
- **C.** that there are many kinds of frogs
- **D.** about the water-holding frog

The correct answer is **C.** The story includes details about three kinds of frogs. These details support the first sentence.

Sometimes a story does not have a main idea sentence. You can figure out the main idea by reading the details. Read the story below.

The Sahara is a desert found in North Africa. The desert gets from 5 to 10 inches of rain per year. Sometimes there are dry periods that last for years. It may reach 135 degrees during the day.

_____ 2. The story mainly tells
- **A.** how hot the Sahara is
- **B.** facts about the Sahara
- **C.** where the Sahara is found
- **D.** how much rainfall the Sahara gets

Read each passage. After each passage you will answer a question about the main idea of the passage. Remember, the main idea is the main point in a story.

1. An iguana is part of the lizard family. Marine iguanas are strange lizards. They are called diving dragons. They jump off rocks and dive into the water to find food. Now scientists have found an amazing fact about marine iguanas. Some can make themselves shrink when food is hard to find! When their food supply returns, they grow back to normal size.

_____ **1.** The story mainly tells

    A. why marine iguanas are strange lizards

    B. what a diving dragon eats

    C. how iguanas shrink

    D. how an iguana finds food

---

2. Buttons are useful. At first buttons were used only as ornaments. Once, a king of France had a coat with thousands of gold buttons sewn on it. Then someone had a new thought. Why not make a slit in cloth and push a button through it? Buttons began to hold pants up and keep shirts closed. Some buttons are tiny works of art. Collectors search for them.

_____ **2.** The story mainly tells

    A. that buttons are useful

    B. where gold buttons were sewn

    C. how shirts stay closed

    D. what collectors search for

3. Horse shows are the place to see beautiful horses. The riders and horses get scores for each event. First all the riders walk their horses around the ring. Then they trot the horses, making them go faster and faster. Finally they gallop. When they jump over logs or ponds, the riders must not fall. The best riders and horses get ribbons and prizes.

_____ **3.** The story mainly tells
- **A.** which kinds of horses jump the highest
- **B.** who gets prizes for galloping
- **C.** what horses and riders do in horse shows
- **D.** how the horses jump fences

4. Many people are afraid of flying in airplanes. Sometimes they're so afraid that they get sick. This is a problem. These people can never visit friends who live far away. Doctors have started classes that teach people about planes. The people practice flying in planes. Many people have learned to get over their fear of flying this way!

_____ **4.** The story mainly tells
- **A.** why people are afraid of the dark
- **B.** how people learn to get over their fear of flying
- **C.** why people are afraid of flying
- **D.** how these people learn to fly airplanes

5. Mayflies are insects. They begin life underwater. As they grow older, mayflies leave the water and grow wings. When their wings are strong, they fly with thousands of other mayflies near the water. You can often see them by ponds. They look like a dark cloud hanging over the water.

_____ **5.** The story mainly tells
- **A.** why mayflies have no wings
- **B.** what looks like a cloud
- **C.** about the life of mayflies
- **D.** how mayflies grow on land

1. Kings and queens had the earliest zoos. They wanted to show off their money by keeping strange animals. Later, people kept animals in zoos because they wanted to learn about them. Students could take classes at the zoo. Today zoos try to help certain animals. These animals are disappearing from their wild homes. Zoos help keep these animals safe.

_____ **1.** The story mainly tells

    A. how rulers showed off their money

    B. which people learned about zoo animals

    C. how zoos have changed over the years

    D. how animals will never disappear

---

2. Some butterflies lay their eggs on just one kind of plant. By tasting the plant, they know which one is right. Sometimes butterflies taste the wrong plant, so they fly to another plant and taste again. When they find the right plant, they lay their eggs there. Soon the eggs hatch. The hungry babies eat the plant their mother chose!

_____ **2.** The story mainly tells

    A. when baby butterflies come out of eggs

    B. how butterflies choose where to lay eggs

    C. what flies from one plant to another

    D. how butterflies always taste the right plant

---

3. Airplanes have changed our lives. Long ago, people traveled in ships. They spent weeks or even months getting from one country to another. Today airplanes carry people halfway around the world in 15 hours. So we spend less time going places and more time doing things.

_____ **3.** The story mainly tells

    A. how small the world was long ago

    B. how fast ships sailed around the world

    C. how airplanes changed our lives

    D. how people still travel on ships

4. A man in Florida can talk to fish. He spent a long time learning how to do this. First he watched fish very closely. Then he listened to the noises they made. Finally he learned to make the same sounds. Sometimes the fish listen to him. At times he can even make them do things. This man thinks that someday fishermen might be able to call fish to their nets.

_____ **4.** The story mainly tells
   A. why fish listen to sounds
   B. who likes to fish
   C. how a man talks to fish
   D. how the fish never listen to this man

---

5. John Chapman planted apple trees in Ohio in the early 1800s. He carried the seeds all over the country. He sold the seeds or just gave them away to people. Chapman was a very kind man. He loved people, animals, and trees. The story of Johnny Appleseed is the story of his life.

_____ **5.** The story mainly tells
   A. how apple trees grow from seeds
   B. where we get the story of Johnny Appleseed
   C. when Chapman lived in Ohio
   D. how Chapman traveled the country

1. Back in the 1700s, people often ate with their fingers. In England, the fourth Earl of Sandwich liked to keep his hands clean. One day he asked to have his food placed between two slices of bread. The sandwich was born. It was a great idea. Without it, lunches might be different today. We could be spreading our peanut butter and jelly on broccoli!

_____ **1.** The story mainly tells
   A. how the sandwich was born
   B. how people used to eat
   C. why lunches might be different
   D. where to put peanut butter

---

2. The first dollhouses were built for grown-ups. These houses were as tall as people. They were also filled with pretty things. Rich people made these dollhouses look like their own homes. Only later did they build smaller dollhouses for children. Some of these are still around. They help us learn what real houses looked like long ago.

_____ **2.** The story mainly tells
   A. when people made dollhouses for children
   B. which dollhouses were the tallest
   C. what the first dollhouses were like
   D. which people didn't build dollhouses

3. Mother ducks take baby ducks away from each other. This is the way it happens. The mother ducks take their babies swimming. Soon the pond is full of ducks. The mother ducks quack. They swim around the baby ducks. The mother duck that quacks loudest gets the greatest number of babies. Some mother ducks may have 40 baby ducks. Others may have only two or three.

_____ **3.** The story mainly tells
     A. which duck quacks the loudest
     B. how mother ducks take babies away
     C. when the ducks go swimming
     D. how baby ducks choose their mother

---

4. Cats are very much like lions and tigers. They can jump high in the air. Cats can jump 7 feet straight up. They have padded feet. That way they can sneak up on their prey. Cats have 18 claws on their feet. They can push out and draw back their claws.

_____ **4.** The story mainly tells
     A. how a cat looks
     B. about special things that a cat can do
     C. how high a cat can jump
     D. why a cat is a better pet than a dog

---

5. Aardvarks are strange animals. They have short stumpy legs and huge donkey ears. Termites are their favorite feast. Aardvarks break open the termites' mounds with their strong claws. Humans would have to use a pickax to break these mounds. Soldier termites try to save the mound by biting the aardvarks, but it is useless. Aardvarks' stiff hair and tough skin help keep them safe.

_____ **5.** The story mainly tells
     A. why aardvarks are strange animals
     B. what aardvarks eat
     C. why soldier termites bite
     D. about aardvarks' stiff hair

1. Children learn their first lessons in banking when they use piggy banks. Children put pennies in their banks and wait for the number of pennies to grow. The money is safe there. When the bank is full, the child can buy something with the money. In the same way, children's parents put their money in a real bank. It's safe there. They can add more money every month. Later they can use it to buy the things they need.

_____ **1.** The story mainly tells
- **A.** how children spend their money
- **B.** how a piggy bank is a lesson in banking
- **C.** when grown people put money in a bank
- **D.** why grown people don't use piggy banks

---

2. Zoo elephants get very good care. Each morning zookeepers give them a special bath. They wash the elephants with water and a brush. Then they paint oil on their skin and rub oil on their feet. This is very important in elephant care. It helps the elephants stay healthy.

_____ **2.** The story mainly tells
- **A.** why zookeepers have happy lives
- **B.** who paints oil on elephants
- **C.** how zookeepers give elephants special care
- **D.** how much elephants eat

---

3. Not long ago, people raised their own chickens. They fed the chickens leftover food. They also gathered fresh eggs every day. Every morning the roosters awakened everybody. Sometimes the family cooked a chicken for dinner. Today life has changed. Most people buy chickens and eggs at stores. They have clocks to wake them.

_____ **3.** The story mainly tells
- **A.** that people once raised chickens
- **B.** why chickens give fresh eggs
- **C.** when the family cooked a chicken
- **D.** where the chicken pens were found

4. All winter long bears do nothing but sleep. To get ready for their winter sleep, they eat. They eat much food to get fat. The fat will become food their bodies will use while they sleep. Bears choose sleeping places such as caves. They might also choose a hollow log or even a big pile of brush. If it gets warm on a winter day, the bears may come out to walk around. They don't stay out long. Only in the spring do they finally get up and look for food.

_____ **4.** The story mainly tells
     A. what kind of life a bear leads
     B. who likes caves for sleeping
     C. where bears sleep in the summer
     D. why bears love honey

5. Many farmers today grow fields of yellow sunflowers. People have many uses for sunflower seeds. After the seeds are dried and salted, people buy them to eat. Some sunflower seeds are pressed to make cooking oil. Some seeds are also ground to make a kind of butter.

_____ **5.** The story mainly tells
     A. why people eat salty seeds
     B. how sunflower seeds are of great value
     C. who uses cooking oil
     D. who likes sunflower butter

1. A new thread is being made from seashells. This thread is very strong. Doctors can use it to fix cuts in people's skin. The thread helps bring the cut skin back together. Also, it never has to be taken out. After some time the thread becomes part of the body.

_____ **1.** The story mainly tells

    A. why thread made of seashells is used to fix cuts

    B. how thread is made into cloth

    C. how cuts in the skin get well

    D. how doctors take out the thread

2. Neil Armstrong was an astronaut. In 1969, he did something no one else had done before. He set foot on the Moon. He said, "That's one small step for a man, one giant leap for mankind." Edwin Aldrin followed Armstrong. They placed an American flag on the Moon.

_____ **2.** The story mainly tells

    A. what Neil Armstrong said on the Moon

    B. who first walked on the Moon

    C. how Armstrong and Aldrin reached the Moon

    D. what clothing Armstrong wore on the Moon

3. Baseball players have to step up to get onto the field. They must step down when their side is out. Their dugouts are built half below the ground. They are made like that for good reasons. If dugouts were tall, the fans who sit behind them could not see the game. Lower dugouts would be a problem for the players. They would need a stepladder to see the game.

_____ **3.** The story mainly tells
- **A.** where baseball players sit
- **B.** when baseball players must step down
- **C.** why dugouts are built the way they are
- **D.** who needs a stepladder

---

4. We all know that babies make funny sounds. Little by little, babies learn that some sounds will call their mother and father. Other sounds will get them food. Yet some sounds will bring them nothing at all. Babies learn to talk by finding out which sounds work best.

_____ **4.** The story mainly tells
- **A.** which babies make the loudest noises
- **B.** how babies learn to talk
- **C.** when babies first start to make noise
- **D.** how babies aren't smart

---

5. Centipedes are not insects, but they look like insects. They are long animals with short legs. *Centipede* means "hundred feet," but centipedes have 350 legs! Millipedes also have many legs. *Millipede* means "thousand feet," but they have about 700 legs!

_____ **5.** The story mainly tells
- **A.** how many legs centipedes and millipedes have
- **B.** what kind of animal a centipede is
- **C.** that centipedes have one hundred legs
- **D.** that millipedes have one thousand legs

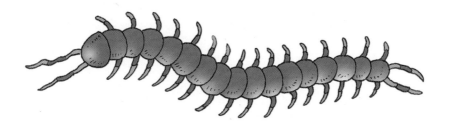

1. The bee hummingbird is the size of a bee. This bird is 2 ½ inches long. It weighs the same as a lump of sugar. It has a long beak. This tiny bird lives in Cuba.

_____ **1.** The story mainly tells
   A. about a kind of bee
   B. how a hummingbird is like a bee
   C. about the smallest insect
   D. about the bee hummingbird

2. One kind of spider makes a web underwater. It weaves its web in water plants. Then it carries bubbles of air down to fill the web. The water spider lies still on its web. Soon a water insect swims near it. The spider dashes out and catches the insect. It brings its catch back to the air-filled web to eat.

_____ **2.** The story mainly tells
   A. what a water spider looks like
   B. how a water spider builds its web
   C. what the spider does with water insects
   D. how one kind of spider lives under the water

3. A fly has six feet. Each foot has a plump little pad on the bottom. The pads flatten out when the fly walks on a smooth surface. They give off a sticky liquid that holds the fly to the wall or the ceiling. The liquid acts like glue so that the fly doesn't fall.

_____ **3.** The story mainly tells
   A. how many legs a fly has
   B. about the fly's special feet
   C. how flies make glue
   D. about different types of flies

4. One day Frank Baum was telling a story to some children. He told about a girl named Dorothy. She was swept from her home to a strange land. It was a magical place. One of the children asked Baum about the name of the strange land. He looked around the room. He saw a filing cabinet. One drawer was labeled A–G. The next was labeled H–N. The last drawer was O–Z. He looked at the last drawer and named the land Oz. Baum later wrote the book *The Wonderful Wizard of Oz.*

_____ **4.** This story mainly tells
    A. how Baum named the land of Oz
    B. where Dorothy lived
    C. how Baum named Dorothy
    D. when Baum wrote *The Wonderful Wizard of Oz*

---

5. A chameleon is a kind of lizard. Its skin is clear, but it can change color. Under its skin are layers of cells. These cells have yellow, black, and red color in them. Anger makes these colors darken. Fear makes them lighten. Fear also makes yellow spots appear. Temperature and light can also cause these colors to change. These changes make the chameleon hard to see, because chameleons change to blend with their surroundings. Changing colors can save a chameleon's life.

_____ **5.** The story mainly tells
    A. that a chameleon has clear skin
    B. how a chameleon's skin can change color
    C. where chameleons live
    D. that sometimes a chameleon has yellow spots

1. Sometimes deep in the ocean, an earthquake shakes the ocean floor. The movement starts a tidal wave. At first the wave is small. But it can move toward the shore at a speed of up to 500 miles per hour. It makes a huge wave as it reaches the coast. The tidal wave hits the land with great force. It can destroy everything in its path.

_____ **1.** The story mainly tells
- **A.** that earthquakes happen on the ocean floor
- **B.** how fast a tidal wave moves
- **C.** another name for a tidal wave
- **D.** how a tidal wave is formed

2. Camels have one or two humps on their backs. The humps are made of fat. The fat stores energy. When there isn't much food, the camel lives off the energy from its humps.

_____ **2.** The story mainly tells
- **A.** about the humps of camels
- **B.** how many humps a camel has
- **C.** how much fat is in a camel's humps
- **D.** how heavy a camel's humps can be

3. A person who sews clothes is a tailor. One kind of bird is good at sewing. This bird is called the tailor bird. It sews a nest for itself. The tailor bird uses its beak to punch holes in the edges of leaves. Then it threads a piece of spiderweb through the holes. It pulls the leaves together and knots the thread. This makes a cup-shaped nest. The tailor bird lines the nest with cotton or grass.

_____ **3.** The story mainly tells
  A. why this bird is called a tailor bird
  B. how the tailor bird lines its nest
  C. what a tailor bird's nest is called
  D. where the tailor bird is found

---

4. Pumice is a rock that can float on water. Pumice is not solid. It has bubbles of air inside. Pumice is formed from lava. Lava is the liquid rock that pours from a volcano. The lava bubbles and then cools to form pumice.

_____ **4.** The story mainly tells
  A. what lava is
  B. how pumice is used
  C. why pumice can float
  D. how pumice looks

---

5. Pigskin is very sensitive. It sunburns very easily. This is why pigs don't lie in the sun. They lie in the shade. They roll around in the mud to cover their skin from the sun.

_____ **5.** The story mainly tells
  A. how pigs keep from getting sunburned
  B. what pigs do in the sun
  C. where pigs live
  D. how pigskin is made

1. Louis XIV, king of France, was a short man. He wanted to look taller, so he ordered high heels for his shoes. Then he had his shoes trimmed with lace, bows, and jewels. One pair of shoes had bows that were 16 inches wide. He had artists paint scenes on the heels of his shoes. Soon other men in France wore high-heeled shoes with flowers and bows.

_____ **1.** The story mainly tells
  A. about King Louis XIV's high heels
  B. how tall King Louis XIV was
  C. how the king painted his heels
  D. about shoes that men wear today

---

2. When an io moth is resting, its wings are folded. If the moth sees a hungry bird, it unfolds its wings. The wings have markings called eyespots. Each spot looks like a big eye. The eyespots scare the bird away.

_____ **2.** The story mainly tells
  A. which animals have eyespots
  B. about the size of eyespots
  C. how an io moth protects itself
  D. about the color of an io moth

---

3. People pick the ripe fruit of the soapberry tree. They cut up the fruit. Then they mix it with cold water from a stream or lake. The fruit fills the water with suds. These suds are used to wash clothes.

_____ **3.** The story mainly tells
  A. where soapberry trees are found
  B. about a natural laundry soap
  C. about the many uses of the soapberry tree
  D. about washing clothes

4. The Loch Ness monster has been seen many times. It lives in a lake in Scotland called Loch Ness. The waters of Loch Ness are the color of coffee. So no one has been able to take a clear picture of the monster or catch it. The monster is said to be about 20 feet long with a tiny head and a long neck. Its big body has flippers and many humps.

_____ **4.** The story mainly tells
   A. that the monster does not exist
   B. how many people have seen the monster
   C. where Loch Ness is located
   D. how no one has proved that the monster is real

---

5. Trees are cut down and chopped into tiny chips. The wood chips are cooked in water and chemicals. They make a pulp that looks like oatmeal. The pulp is squeezed until it is very thin and flat. It is dried to make a giant sheet of paper. Paper can also be made from cotton fibers.

_____ **5.** The story mainly tells
   A. how paper is made
   B. what wood pulp is
   C. how many trees it takes to make a sheet of paper
   D. how cotton fibers are turned into paper

Writing Roundup

Read each story. Think about the main idea. Write the main idea in your own words.

1. Mary Myers liked to go up in balloons. She wanted to be her own pilot. In 1880 she did just that. Her balloon took off from Little Falls, New York. Mary became the first woman balloon pilot. After that many women flew alone in their own balloons.

What is the main idea of this story?

_____

_____

2. Beto lived in the city. One summer he visited his Uncle Alex on the farm. That summer Beto learned how to ride horses. Now Beto is grown up. He rides horses in races. He is a famous jockey. He says he owes it all to his Uncle Alex.

What is the main idea of this story?

_____

_____

3. People have learned much about the oceans. They learned through exploring oceans. Oceans are huge, and they are very deep. There is much more to learn. There still are many questions about life in the oceans.

What is the main idea of this story?

_____

_____

Prewriting

Think of a main idea that you would like to write about, such as visiting a farm, flying in a balloon, or exploring the ocean. Fill in the chart below.

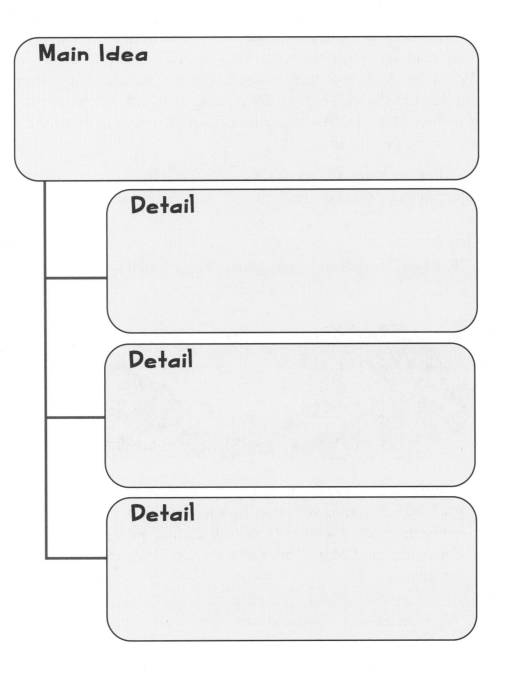

Main Idea

Detail

Detail

Detail

On Your Own

Now use another sheet of paper to write your story.
Underline the sentence that tells the main idea.

What Is a Conclusion?

A conclusion is a decision you make after thinking about what you have read. In a story the writer may not state all of his or her ideas. When you read, you often have to hunt for clues so that you can understand the whole story. By putting all of the writer's clues together, you can draw a conclusion about something that the writer has not stated.

There are many stories in this unit. You will draw conclusions based on each story that you read.

Try It!

Read this story about a rain forest. Think about what it tells you.

The climate around the equator is always warm. Much of the land is covered with rain forests. It rains in these areas every day. Some land gets more than 500 inches per year. September and March are the wettest and warmest times of the year.

What conclusion can you draw? Write your conclusion on the lines.

_____

_____

You may have written something such as, "It is warm and wet in the rain forests" or "It is never cold in the rain forests." You can draw these conclusions from the paragraph. The first sentence tells about the warm climate around the equator. The second sentence says that it rains every day. From those clues, you can draw these conclusions.

Using What You Know

Let's say that animals can talk. Several animals are describing themselves in the stories below. Hunt for clues that tell which animal is talking. Answer the questions by writing the name of each animal.

I have black-and-white stripes. The horse is my cousin. I live in a herd and like to graze on grass. I live on the huge plains of Africa. When I'm frightened, I run away as fast as I can. I can run 40 miles per hour.

What am I? _____

I'm the largest animal on land. I weigh 250 pounds at birth. I'm gray and have large ears. I'm also one of the smartest animals. I live in a group. If a member of my group gets hurt, I try to help. I eat and drink with my long trunk.

What am I? _____

I'm the tallest animal in the world. I could easily look into your second-story window. My long neck lets me eat the fruit and leaves that no other animal can reach. Lions, cheetahs, and hyenas are my enemies.

What am I? _____

I live in the ocean. The whale is my cousin. I have a long, pointed nose. I'm very intelligent, and I'm friendly to people. In fact, sometimes I even let people ride on my back. I'm playful and like to learn tricks. I'm often trained to perform for crowds.

What am I? _____

Read each passage. After each passage you will answer a question that will require you to draw a conclusion about the story. Remember, a conclusion is a decision you make after putting together all the clues you are given.

1. Baseball is a big sport in Japan. The rules are the same as those in America, but the customs are different. Players in Japan don't show their anger when they're *out*. They don't try to hurt the player from the other team as the player slides into second base. Also, when the fans clap, the players bow to them.

_____ **1.** From this story you can tell that
  A. Japanese players do not slide into second base
  B. American players show their anger
  C. Japanese players can play better
  D. Japanese players wave when the fans clap

2. The knight in chess is different from the other pieces. The knight is the only piece that can jump over the other ones. This move comes from the days of the knights. Knights traveled far and wide in search of adventure. They traveled off the regular road. There they often met enemies. The knight in chess also does not have a regular move. The knight's move in chess is like the life of the knight of long ago.

_____ **2.** From this story you can tell that
  A. all chess pieces move in the same way
  B. the knight in chess has a regular move
  C. chess pieces move in different ways
  D. the knight in chess does not move

3. How fast can you run? At top speed a human can run about 20 miles per hour. A snake can travel 2 miles per hour. The fastest mammal is the cheetah. It can run up to 70 miles per hour. A golden eagle can fly 120 miles per hour, and a duck hawk can fly up to 180 miles per hour.

_____ **3.** From this story you can tell that
  A. eagles fly faster than duck hawks
  B. snakes move very fast
  C. cheetahs run faster than humans
  D. humans are the fastest mammals

4. Years ago in England, many people became sick. Nobody knew why. Then a doctor found out that all the sick people lived near each other. He noticed that they all drank water from the same water well. The doctor took the handle off the well pump. People could no longer draw and drink the water. Suddenly they stopped getting sick.

_____ **4.** From this story you can tell that
  A. everyone in England got sick
  B. the doctors at that time were not very smart
  C. the water was making the people sick
  D. there weren't enough doctors to help the sick

5. Long ago, Spanish ships sailed to America. They landed in a warm part of the country. The sun shone brightly there. Flowers bloomed even in the winter. There wasn't any snow. The Spanish people called the land Florida. It is the Spanish word for "blooming." That's how the state got its name.

_____ **5.** From this story you can tell that
  A. American states can have Spanish names
  B. the Spanish people came in the spring
  C. *Florida* means "snow" in Spanish
  D. the Spanish ships landed in Texas

1. About 200 years ago, a doctor climbed a mountain in Europe. In those days people never climbed mountains. They did not know what the tops of mountains were like. In fact they thought the doctor would meet many terrible monsters along the way. He came back down, safe and sound. He hadn't seen a single monster. Today many people enjoy the sport of mountain climbing.

_____ **1.** From this story you can tell that
    A. there are monsters living on mountains
    B. there were trees on top of the mountain
    C. others began climbing mountains after the doctor returned
    D. the doctor was hurt during his climb

2. Ants help keep one tree in South America safe. This tree has thorns that are hollow. The ants live inside the thorns. When animals try to eat the tree's leaves, the ants rush out from the thorns. Hundreds of ants bite the animal. The thorns also stick the animal until it moves away.

_____ **2.** From this story you can tell that
    A. the tree and the ants need each other
    B. ants eat other animals for food
    C. the tree in this story is very tall
    D. the thorns don't hurt the animals

3. Long ago in Europe, there were no police. Instead there were only town watchpersons. A watchperson walked the streets at night. Troublemakers stayed away. A watchperson walked for a length of time called a watch. Then someone else took over the next watch. How did a watchperson know when to stop walking? The watchperson carried a small clock. Today the name of the small clock reminds us of the watchpersons of Europe.

_____ **3.** From this story you can tell that
    A. a length of time was called a _stretch_
    B. the name of the clock is _timer_
    C. the name of the clock is _watch_
    D. the watchpersons ran races on the streets

4. Baby Dee woke up and started crying loudly. Scott ran to her from the kitchen. He held Dee and talked to her. Scott didn't know why she was crying. He had fed Dee earlier. He checked to see if the baby's clothes were wet. They were dry. Then Scott noticed an open safety pin lying in Dee's bed.

_____ **4.** From this story you can tell that
    A. the baby was probably very hungry
    B. the safety pin probably hurt Dee
    C. Scott had to take care of only one child
    D. Scott was not a good father

---

5. The largest fish on Earth is the whale shark. This giant shark can grow twice as large as an elephant. The whale shark can weigh up to 12 tons. This shark is big, but it is not harmful to people. It stays alive by eating only small water plants and animals.

_____ **5.** The story suggests that the whale shark
    A. is larger than an elephant
    B. attacks people
    C. is smaller than an elephant
    D. is not a fish

1. Many people don't like bugs. Some bugs bite or sting people. Other bugs eat people's plants and fruits. People poison bugs to get rid of them. Now scientists are finding new ways to kill bugs with germs. The germs make the bugs sick, and then they die. Scientists also use some bugs to fight the other bugs. The ladybug is an example. It eats bugs that hurt fruit.

_____ **1.** From this story you can tell that
   A. poison is not the only way to get rid of bugs
   B. people need to stay away from ladybugs
   C. most bugs like to eat fruit trees
   D. the germs make the bugs stronger

---

2. Laughing makes people feel great. Some people think that laughing is the best thing in life. Now scientists have shown that laughing is good for the body too. Laughing makes the heart beat faster. It brings more air into the body. Many people keep fit by running, but laughing is easier on the feet!

_____ **2.** From this story you can tell that
   A. laughing is good for your health
   B. swimming is very good for your body
   C. crying is like laughing
   D. laughing makes the heart beat slower

3. Mark Twain was a famous writer. One night he was going to give a talk in a small town. He went to the barbershop to get a shave. The barber asked, "Are you going to hear that famous writer tonight? It's sold out, you know. If you go, you'll have to stand."

"Just my luck," said Twain. "I always have to stand when that man gives a talk!"

_____ **3.** From this story you can tell that
  A. the barber did not like to hear writers talk
  B. the barber wasn't going to the talk
  C. the barber didn't know he was shaving Twain
  D. the barber only cut hair

4. How do people put out forest fires? Machines are used to knock down trees that aren't burning. Other machines remove the fallen trees. This clears some of the land. The fire can't cross this land because there is nothing to burn. The firefighters also start small fires nearby to clear more land. Airplanes help to put out the bigger fires by pouring clay on them.

_____ **4.** From this story you can tell that
  A. it is easy to stop a big fire
  B. clay burns very easily when it gets hot
  C. there are many ways to fight forest fires
  D. firefighters make big fires to clear more land

5. Have you ever heard people call money by the name of _bits_? There was once a Mexican coin called a bit. It was worth 12 ½ cents. This coin was also used in parts of the United States. So the people began calling American coins by the name of bits too. Today a quarter is sometimes known as two bits. A half-dollar is called four bits.

_____ **5**. From this story you can conclude that
  A. Mexican coins are used in the United States
  B. today a bit is worth less than a nickel
  C. the name of the Mexican coin is still used for money
  D. Mexican coins are now used for horse bridles

1. Did you know you can start a campfire with ice? First find a large piece of very clear ice. Then melt it down in the palms of your hands. When it is ready, the ice should look like a lens. It should have smooth curves on both sides. Finally use the ice to direct the sun's rays onto paper or wood shavings. This will start the fire.

_____ **1.** The story suggests that
  A. ice burns
  B. the ice will freeze the fire
  C. the warmth of your hands melts the ice
  D. the ice should be curved on one side only

2. Nat Love was a special breed of man. He was a restless cowboy who helped settle the Wild West. As a young man, Love was a slave in Tennessee. Set free by the Civil War, Love learned to herd cattle. In Deadwood, South Dakota, Love won a big cowboy contest. There he gained his nickname, Deadwood Dick.

_____ **2.** You can tell from the story that Nat Love
  A. drove a fast car
  B. was a slave all his life
  C. grew up in Texas
  D. was a skilled cowboy

3. For years people longed to fly in space. They wanted to visit the Moon. In 1957, the Soviet Union launched a satellite. Its name was _Sputnik_. The name means "fellow wayfarer." _Sputnik_ was the first spacecraft to orbit Earth. _Sputnik_ had no crew. But it paved the way for later spaceflights.

_____ **3.** The story tells that _Sputnik_
  A. was the first satellite in space
  B. crashed when it was launched
  C. was full of potatoes
  D. was launched by South Dakota

4. Most whales survive by eating small sea creatures known as krill. Some companies were planning to harvest krill. Mary Cahoon and Mary McWhinnie were afraid that this harvest would cause whales to starve. They went to the South Pole to study the problem. They were the first women to spend a whole winter at the cold South Pole.

_____ **4.** The story suggests that the companies
  A. planned to harvest wheat
  B. weren't worried about whales
  C. liked warm weather
  D. went ice-skating often

5. Some early Native American tribes used adobe to build homes. Adobe is a sun-dried brick made of soil and straw. First they mixed soil and water to make mud. Next they added straw for strength. Then they put the mixture into a brick-shaped mold. Finally the brick was placed in the sun to dry. The dried bricks were used to build the walls of houses.

_____ **5.** From the story you can tell that adobe
  A. was made from concrete
  B. contained straw that weakened the brick
  C. was placed in the rain to dry
  D. was a useful building material

1. The water made a splashing sound as it ran past the big gray rocks. In some places it formed little pools. A small branch bobbed by as the water hurried down the hill. A skunk sat on the mossy bank and watched.

_____ **1.** You can tell that the skunk is sitting near
    A. a bathtub
    B. a fountain
    C. a stream
    D. a lake

2. Flo and Mike were at the animal shelter. Flo wanted a kitten. Mike wanted a puppy. "Cats are cleaner," said Flo. "You don't have to give them baths or take them for walks." Mike didn't care about that. He thought that cats sleep too much to be good playmates.

_____ **2.** This story does <u>not</u> tell
    A. what Flo wanted
    B. what Mike wanted
    C. why Flo likes cats better than dogs
    D. what Flo and Mike decided to get

3. When Tony woke up, he looked out the window. What luck! The mountain was covered with snow. Quickly he pulled on his long underwear and other warm clothes. He ate a good, hot breakfast so that he'd have plenty of energy. Then he checked his equipment. He clomped in his heavy boots toward the door and looked at the slopes.

_____ **3.** In this story the mood is
  A. angry
  B. dangerous
  C. happy
  D. silly

4. Nina was walking down a long hall. She kept turning corners and looking for a certain door. But all the doors she found were the wrong ones. Suddenly a bell rang, and Nina thought, "Oh, I must run or I'll be late." But the bell kept ringing, and Nina couldn't run. Instead, she opened her eyes. The telephone beside her bed was ringing loudly.

_____ **4.** From this story you can tell that
  A. the telephone woke Nina from her dream
  B. Nina was in school
  C. Nina didn't want to answer the telephone
  D. Nina was glad the telephone rang

5. A dog was carrying a bone in his mouth. As he walked over a bridge, he saw his reflection in the water. He thought it was another dog with another bone. "I'll bark and scare that dog away," he thought. "Then I'll have two bones!" After the dog barked, he found out that it doesn't pay to be greedy.

_____ **5.** The dog learned his lesson when
  A. the other dog ran away
  B. he had no bone at all
  C. he went home with a bone
  D. he jumped off the bridge

1. A popular part of Yellowstone Park is Old Faithful. This geyser shoots out thousands of gallons of steam and water every hour. The water is heated deep in the ground. It works its way up through cracks in the ground. Then it bursts high into the air. Yellowstone Park has more geysers than anyplace else on Earth.

_____ **1.** You <u>cannot</u> tell from the story
    A. how often Old Faithful erupts
    B. where Old Faithful can be found
    C. how the water shoots from a geyser
    D. where Yellowstone Park is located

2. Evelyn Cheesman loved to study bugs. She worked as a helper in the Insect House at the London Zoo. In the 1920s she began to go on field trips. Most of her trips were to Asia. During her life she was able to collect 40,000 insects.

_____ **2.** The story suggests that Evelyn Cheesman
    A. was afraid of insects
    B. made most of her field trips to Africa
    C. worked with insects all her life
    D. did not collect insects

3. A great white building stands in Agra, India. It is called the Taj Mahal. It was built by a ruler named Shah Jahan. He wanted a special place to bury his dead wife. Twenty thousand men worked for 20 years to build the Taj Mahal.

_____ **3.** You can tell that the Taj Mahal
    A. was built to be a grave
    B. is found in Indiana
    C. was built of granite
    D. took 30 years to build

4. Lewis Latimer was an African American man. When he was young, he learned the skill of drafting. Then he met Alexander Bell. Bell invented the telephone. He used a design drawn by Latimer. Not long after that, Latimer invented a special lamp. It was called the Latimer Lamp. Later he worked with the great inventor Thomas Edison.

_____ **4.** The story does <u>not</u> tell if Lewis Latimer
A. learned drafting
B. invented more than one thing
C. worked with Thomas Edison
D. invented a special lamp

5. Rosita put the flag up in front of her home. She had read about the correct way to do this. She knew that the flag can be flown from the top of a flag pole. She didn't have a flag pole, though. She also knew that the flag can be hung on a staff. That was how Rosita flew the flag.

_____ **5.** From this story you can tell that
A. Rosita's flag is new
B. Rosita lives in an apartment
C. there is more than one right way to fly a flag
D. Rosita lives in a house

1. There was war in the Middle East. The country of Israel had just been formed. Its Arab neighbors were upset. Ralph Bunche worked in the State Department of the United States. He was sent to help end the war. Bunche knew the war would not be easy to stop. At last he gained peace between the two sides. In 1950, he became the first African American to win the Nobel Peace Prize.

_____ **1.** You can tell from the story that Bunche
   A. worked for the Israeli government
   B. was honored for his hard work
   C. solved the Middle East conflict easily
   D. did not go to the Middle East

2. The Iditarod is a sled-dog race across Alaska. Each team has one person to drive the sled and a group of about 12 dogs to pull it. The person, called a musher, rides on the sled with the food and supplies. The team must cross more than 1,000 miles in cold and often snowy weather. It takes about two weeks. The musher puts special socks on each dog's paws. The musher also feeds and cares for the dogs on the long ride. The dogs run fast and pull the musher all the way to the finish line.

_____ **2.** The story tells that
   A. mushers and their dogs work together to finish the race
   B. sled dogs take care of themselves during the race
   C. mushers don't worry about the sled dogs
   D. mushers and dogs ride on the sled together

3. Leonardo da Vinci was a great artist. He lived about 500 years ago. His most famous work is the painting *Mona Lisa*. He also liked to learn about all sorts of things. He knew much about the human body. He loved to invent things, too. He even drew plans for a flying machine.

_____ **3.** You <u>cannot</u> tell from the story
   A. when Leonardo lived
   B. the name of Leonardo's most famous painting
   C. if Leonardo's flying machine could fly
   D. that Leonardo was a famous painter

4. In Aztec legends the new world needed light and warmth. Two sons of the Aztec god wanted to jump into the fire. They wanted to become the Sun. The first brother jumped into the fire. He became the Sun. But the other brother was afraid. When he jumped into the fire, he became only the Moon.

_____ **4.** The story suggests that
   A. fear kept one brother from becoming the Sun
   B. the Aztec god had five sons
   C. only one brother jumped into the fire
   D. the first brother never jumped into the fire

5. The smallest flower on Earth is on the duckweed plant. Its blossom can barely be seen with the naked eye. The small duckweed plants float free on still water. These plants are a popular food for ducks.

_____ **5.** From the story you <u>cannot</u> tell
   A. on what plant the smallest flower grows
   B. what animal likes to eat the duckweed plant
   C. how small these flowers are
   D. what color the smallest flowers are

1. It is almost spring. Latwanda is not looking forward to the change of season. That is because some flowering plants make her sick. In the spring the air is full of pollens. When Latwanda starts sneezing, her friends know that spring is here.

_____ **1.** This story suggests that
  A. Latwanda catches colds from her friends
  B. pollens make Latwanda sneeze
  C. dust mites make Latwanda sneeze
  D. medicine helps Latwanda get well

2. Tina called her friend Eva in Maryland. Eva sounded very sleepy when she said hello. The two girls talked for 10 minutes. Then Eva said she had to go. "School starts early, you know," she said. "I need my sleep." It was then that Tina knew what she had done. She forgot that Maryland's time zone was not the same as California's.

_____ **2.** You can conclude from the story that
  A. Eva did not enjoy talking to Tina
  B. Tina did not enjoy talking to Eva
  C. Tina and Eva talk often on the phone
  D. Eva was asleep when Tina called

3. Stars do not last forever. After billions of years, they just burn out. Some stars suddenly brighten before they dim. These stars are called novas. *Nova* means "new" in Latin. The novas seem to be new stars. The last great nova was in 1054. It could be seen even in the daytime. It outshone everything in the sky except the Sun and Moon.

_____ **3.** You can tell from the story that
  A. novas are not seen very often
  B. great novas happen all the time
  C. all stars become novas
  D. the nova of 1054 was not very bright

4. Mary Bethune had a dream. She wanted to start a school for African American children. She had a teaching degree, but she had no building, and she had no money. Still Mary had hope. She received donations. At last her school opened in 1904. Through her hard work, the school was a big success. It became known as Bethune-Cookman College. The school, located in Florida, is still open.

_____ **4.** The story does <u>not</u> tell
- **A.** what Mary Bethune's dream was
- **B.** when Mary Bethune's school opened
- **C.** where Mary Bethune's school was located
- **D.** who gave Mary Bethune donations

5. There are more than six billion people on Earth. But scientists think there are four billion insects in each square mile of land. That means there are more than 150 million insects for each person. Luckily, very few insects harm people.

_____ **5.** This story does <u>not</u> tell
- **A.** how many people are on Earth
- **B.** how many insects are in each square mile
- **C.** which insects are most dangerous to people
- **D.** how many more insects there are than people

Writing Roundup

Read each story. Think about a conclusion you can draw. Write your conclusion in a complete sentence.

1. The first movie with people talking was shown in 1927. It was a big hit. Some movies made after that did not have talking in them. Some people still wanted to see the kind of movies they had been watching for years.

What conclusion can you draw from this story?

_____

_____

_____

2. A family in England got a goldfish in 1956. It lived until 1999. One book claims it lived longer than any other goldfish kept in a fish tank. Who knows if that's true? Some people may want to keep the age of their goldfish a secret.

What conclusion can you draw from this story?

_____

_____

3. By the year 2000, 34 Super Bowls had been played. This football game draws big crowds, but many more football fans watch it on television. The game that had the most TV watchers was Super Bowl 16. In it, San Francisco beat Cincinnati.

What conclusion can you draw from this story?

_____

_____

Read the story below. What conclusions can you draw? Use the clues in the story to answer the questions in complete sentences.

Raul is from Cuba. He came to America with his mom. At first they lived in Florida. Raul liked Florida. He did not want to move, but his mom found out she had an uncle in New Jersey. He helped her find a good job. Raul and his mom moved in with Raul's granduncle. Raul went to high school. There he got a surprise. Many of the students were Cuban Americans. They spoke Spanish and English. Raul decided he was going to like New Jersey.

1. Was Raul born in America? How do you know?

_____

_____

2. When Raul lived in Cuba, did he meet his granduncle? How do you know?

_____

_____

3. Do Raul and his mom live alone? How do you know?

_____

_____

4. Does Raul want to move back to Florida? How do you know?

_____

_____

unit 6

What Is an Inference?

An inference is a guess you make after thinking about what you already know. Suppose a friend invites you to a picnic. From what you know about picnics, you might infer that there will be food and drinks, and that you will eat outside.

An author does not write every detail in a story. If every detail were told, a story would be long and boring, and the main point would be lost. Suppose you read, "Lynn went to a restaurant." The writer does not have to tell you what a restaurant is. You already know that it is a place where people go to eat a meal. From what you know, you might imagine that Lynn looked at a menu. Then a server took her order. By filling in these missing details, you could infer that Lynn went to the restaurant to eat. You can infer this by putting together what you read and what you already know.

Try It!

Read this story. Think about the facts in the story.

Earthquakes can cause a lot of damage. This is especially true in places where the soil is loose and damp. An earthquake can turn loose, damp soil into thick mud. Buildings will sink or fall down. Many people may be hurt.

What can you infer? Write an inference on the line below.

_____

_____

You may have written something such as, "An earthquake can harm a city." You can make this inference from what the story tells you about earthquakes and what you already know.

Practice Making Inferences

In lessons 1 through 4 of this unit, you will be asked to answer the question, "Which of these sentences is probably true?" Read the following story and answer the question.

Red-crowned cranes are beautiful birds. They are known for their trumpeting call. Many of these cranes live on an island in Japan. They live in marshes and are protected by law, but there are fewer than 2,000 cranes left. They are in danger of disappearing.

___B___ **1.** Which of these sentences is probably true?
   A. The Japanese don't care about these cranes.
   B. People in Japan want to help the cranes.
   C. Red-crowned cranes live in the desert.
   D. There are too many cranes in Japan.

Answer **B** is the best choice. The story says that these cranes are protected by law. From the story you can infer that people in Japan want to help these cranes.

In lessons 5 through 8 of this unit you will do a new kind of exercise. Each story is followed by statements. Some of the statements are inferences. Others are facts. Decide whether each statement is an inference or a fact.

Ben moved from England to Maine. In England he was taught to stand up when answering a question. In his new class, he stood up when the teacher called on him. Some of the other students laughed at him. After class the teacher told him that he could stay in his seat when she called on him.

Fact	Inference		
○	●	**2. A.**	Ben was a polite person.
●	○	**B.**	Ben moved from England to Maine.
○	●	**C.**	The teacher wanted to help Ben.
●	○	**D.**	Some students laughed at Ben.

You can find statements **B** and **D** in the story, so they are facts. We can infer from the way he acts that Ben is a polite person, but this isn't stated in the story. So **A** is an inference. We can guess from the teacher's actions that she wanted to help Ben. So **C** is also an inference.

Read the passages. Use what you know about inference to answer the questions. Remember, an inference is a guess you make by putting together what you know and what you read or see in the stories.

1. John loved to fish. He went fishing anytime he could. The weather was very hot and dry. John sat on the shore, thinking about catching fish. All day John waited patiently. The fish just would not bite. He was hungry and thirsty, but did not move even as the Sun went down.

_____ **1.** Which of these sentences is probably true?
   A. There were no fish in the water.
   B. John wanted to stay until he caught a fish.
   C. Other people were fishing at the pond.
   D. John went home early for dinner.

2. The village people chose a boy to guard the sheep. It was an important job. If a wolf came near, the boy was supposed to call the people in the village. Then they would come to help him. The boy watched the sheep for a little while. Then he decided to have some fun. He cried out loudly, "Wolf! Wolf!" The people rushed out to fight the wolf. When they arrived the boy was laughing at them. There was no wolf.

_____ **2.** Which of these sentences is probably true?
   A. Everyone thought the joke was funny.
   B. Several of the sheep got lost.
   C. The people were angry at the boy.
   D. The boy was very kind.

3. You have probably seen a rainbow in the sky. What does it take to form a rainbow? There are three conditions for a rainbow to form. First, there must be many raindrops in the sky. Second, the sunlight must be shining on the raindrops. Third, the Sun must be behind you. Then the rainbow will be in front of you.

_____ **3.** Which of these sentences is probably true?
- **A.** Rainbows are only seen in the West.
- **B.** Rainbows always appear during storms.
- **C.** Rainbows never appear when there are clouds.
- **D.** Rainbows rarely appear at night.

---

4. A pet store owner in Maine noticed a strange thing. He found that he could tell when the country was having good times or bad. He looked at what kind of dogs people wanted to buy. People bought small dogs when they had enough money. People bought big dogs when they felt sad or needed protection.

_____ **4.** Which of these sentences is probably true?
- **A.** People bought big dogs during bad times.
- **B.** Pet store owners don't like dogs.
- **C.** People bought big dogs during good times.
- **D.** Dogs make better pets than cats do.

---

5. The cowbird does not build a nest of its own. The mother cowbird lays her eggs in the nest of another bird. Then the cowbird leaves the eggs. She hopes the other bird will take care of her babies when they hatch.

_____ **5.** Which of these sentences is probably true?
- **A.** The cowbird is lazy.
- **B.** Nests are easy to build.
- **C.** The cowbird is very caring.
- **D.** Baby cowbirds eat much food.

1. The Pyramids in Egypt were built more than 5,000 years ago. The Pyramids are made of large blocks of stone. They are stacked on top of each other. The blocks are very heavy. People moved the blocks by placing logs under them. The logs acted like wheels to make the blocks easier to move. The stones were then pulled into place.

_____ **1.** Which of these sentences is probably true?
   A. The Pyramids in Egypt are very old.
   B. The Pyramids were built from large trees.
   C. Large rocks are easy to move.
   D. The Pyramids were discovered recently.

2. The day was sunny and hot. Ava stood happily at the side of the swimming pool. She thought about the clear, blue water. Then she jumped in. As she began swimming, she started shaking, and her skin began to turn blue.

_____ **2.** Which of these sentences is probably true?
   A. The water was very hot.
   B. Ava forgot to wear her coat.
   C. The water was very cold.
   D. Ava didn't know how to swim.

3. Fingernails grow faster on the right hand of people who are right-handed. The nails grow faster on the left hand of left-handed people. They grow faster in the day than at night. Ray has to trim the nails on his left hand more than the ones on his right hand.

_____ **3.** Which of these sentences is probably true?
   A. Ray is a right-handed person.
   B. Painted nails grow very slowly.
   C. Ray is a left-handed person.
   D. At night Ray's nails grow quickly.

4. One day Sam found a library book under his bed. He realized he was late in taking it back. Sam decided to return the book the next day. The next day, he could not find the book. Two days later Sam found the book again, so he hurried to the library. When he arrived, there was a sign on the door. He walked home again with the book in his hand.

_____ **4.** Which of these sentences is probably true?
  A. Sam didn't like the book very much.
  B. The book could move by itself.
  C. Sam did not know where the library was.
  D. When Sam went to the library, it was closed.

5. One day Ann heard her friend Tom talking. Tom was telling everybody how smart his dog was. Tom said his dog could do tricks and could even ride a bicycle. Ann knew that Tom's dog was just like any other dog. Ann just smiled as Tom went on talking.

_____ **5.** Which of these sentences is probably true?
  A. Ann didn't understand Tom's story.
  B. Tom wanted to make Ann mad at him.
  C. Ann didn't want to hurt Tom's feelings.
  D. Tom had two dogs and a cat.

1. Nick sat trembling behind the couch as a storm roared outside. Lightning flashed and thunder rumbled. Each time the thunder rolled, Nick screamed loudly. Nick's dad tried to get the boy to come out, but Nick would not move.

_____ **1.** Which of these sentences is probably true?
   A. Storms made Nick's dad afraid.
   B. Nick liked to play hide and seek.
   C. Nick's dad made him feel better.
   D. Nick was afraid of thunder and lightning.

---

2. Bill Stanton found a skunk in his garage. He asked the city of Chicago for help. He wanted to get rid of the skunk, but the city would not help him. Bill bought a trap to catch the skunk himself. Then he learned he had broken the law several times. First he had brought a trap into the city. Then he had trapped an animal without the city's permission. The city laws stated that he could not keep the skunk in his garage. They also said he could not kill the skunk or let it go free, either!

_____ **2.** Which of these sentences is probably true?
   A. The skunk became Bill's best friend.
   B. Bill didn't know what to do with the skunk.
   C. The skunk was moved to the city leaders' office.
   D. Bill was glad the skunk was in his garage.

3. The sport of softball began as indoor baseball. The first game of softball was played on a cold day in November 1887. It took place in a Chicago boat club. The men used an old boxing glove for a ball and a broomstick for a bat.

_____ **3.** Which of these sentences is probably true?
  A. The men wanted to play baseball in the winter.
  B. Real baseballs cost a lot of money in 1887.
  C. The men didn't know how to play baseball.
  D. People first played softball outside.

4. When you think of dinosaurs, you likely think of large animals. Not all dinosaurs were large. The smallest dinosaurs were about the size of a chicken. They were fast runners. They probably ate insects, frogs, and lizards.

_____ **4.** Which of these sentences is probably true?
  A. Dinosaurs were many different sizes.
  B. Dinosaurs ate only plants.
  C. Some dinosaurs looked like chickens.
  D. Dinosaurs were all about the same size.

5. The speed limit on the road was 30 miles per hour. But drivers always went faster than that. The neighbors who lived on the road were angry about the speeders. So they talked to the city leaders. The leaders soon took action. They raised the speed limit to 35 miles per hour.

_____ **5.** Which of these sentences is probably true?
  A. The neighbors disliked the new speed limit.
  B. The neighbors were glad the leaders took action.
  C. After hearing the leaders' decision, the neighbors moved away.
  D. Drivers started going 30 miles per hour.

1. Bob Hope was playing golf with a friend. His friend missed an easy shot. The angry friend threw his golf club into the tall grass. Bob secretly got the golf club back and started using it himself. Bob hit the ball a long way with his friend's club. The friend thought Bob's golf club was very good. He offered to buy it for $50. Bob sold the man the club he had just thrown away. Later Bob told his friend what had happened.

_____ **1.** Which of these sentences is probably true?
A. Bob decided to keep his friend's golf club.
B. Bob's friend felt silly for buying back his own club.
C. Bob used the money to open a golf shop.
D. Bob's friend never played golf again.

2. The president was coming to visit the small town. Everyone was very excited. All the people worked hard to clean up their town. They mowed the grass and swept the sidewalks. They fixed up the old houses. They even painted the water tower.

_____ **2.** Which of these sentences is probably true?
A. The president was moving to the town.
B. The people were trying to fool the president.
C. The president only liked big towns.
D. The people wanted their town to look nice.

3. Jim carefully lifted the eggs from their box. He handed two eggs to his mother. Then Jim measured a cup of milk, being careful not to spill any. He rubbed the pan with butter and watched as his mother poured in the batter. Then Jim and his mother cleaned up.

_____ **3.** Which of these sentences is probably true?
A. Jim was a good helper.
B. Jim's mother was a bad cook.
C. Jim was hungry.
D. Jim's mother was lazy.

4. Jan was always playing basketball. In fact, she almost never left the basketball court. Jan started practicing early every morning. As the Sun went down, Jan was still bouncing the basketball.

_____ **4.** Which of these sentences is probably true?
  A. Jan slept at the basketball court.
  B. Tennis was very important to Jan.
  C. Jan wanted to be a great basketball player.
  D. The basketball was too big to bounce inside.

---

5. When he was a boy, George Washington Carver had a garden. He loved to study the plants and flowers growing there. He knew how to make the flowers bloom. George could also cure sick plants. People began to call him the "plant doctor."

_____ **5.** Which of these sentences is probably true?
  A. George became a plant scientist later in life.
  B. The neighbors didn't like George's garden.
  C. George chopped down all the plants.
  D. His mother called George the "animal doctor."

1. People have been eating cheese for more than 4,000 years. Cheese is made from milk. As milk turns to cheese, solid clumps form. When the liquid is taken out, the cheese becomes even harder. The cheese is then allowed to *age*. This means it has to sit for a while before it's ready. Sometimes the cheese is ready to be eaten in two weeks. For other types of cheese, aging takes up to two years.

Fact	Inference	
○	○	**1. A.** Cheese is made from milk.
○	○	**B.** There are different kinds of cheeses.
○	○	**C.** Aging cheese can take two years.
○	○	**D.** Cheese hardens when liquid is removed.

2. Have you ever caught fireflies on a warm summer night? Fireflies are interesting little insects. They make light with their bodies, but the light is not hot. Fireflies use their lights to send signals to other fireflies.

Fact	Inference	
○	○	**2. A.** Fireflies come out in summer.
○	○	**B.** The light of fireflies is not hot.
○	○	**C.** Fireflies send signals with their lights.
○	○	**D.** Fireflies can only send signals at night.

3. If you watch the sky at night, you may see a shooting star. Shooting stars are actually meteors. Meteors are small bits of rock that enter the atmosphere. When this happens, they burn up. They look like streaks of light. Sometimes Earth passes through a place with many small rocks. When this happens, the sky is filled with meteors. Since there are so many meteors, these events are called meteor showers.

Fact	Inference	
○	○	**3. A.** Meteors are small bits of rock.
○	○	**B.** Meteors are not really stars.
○	○	**C.** Most meteors never reach the ground.
○	○	**D.** Meteor showers are made up of many meteors.

4. Drew's team was tied with the other soccer team. The game was almost over. Drew had scored all his team's goals in the game so far. His friend Brian had never scored a goal. As Drew ran up the field, he saw that Brian was in a great position to kick the ball into the goal. Drew quickly kicked the ball to Brian.

Fact	Inference	
○	○	**4. A.** Drew wanted Brian to make a goal.
○	○	**B.** Drew was a thoughtful person.
○	○	**C.** Drew was a good soccer player.
○	○	**D.** Brian had never scored a goal.

5. Mount St. Helens is a volcano in Washington. In 1980, it erupted for the first time in more than 100 years. Fire and melting rock poured out of the volcano. This caused rivers to flood. Four states were covered with ash. More than 60 people were killed.

Fact	Inference	
○	○	**5. A.** Mount St. Helens erupted in 1980.
○	○	**B.** The volcano did not erupt often.
○	○	**C.** People lived near Mount St. Helens.
○	○	**D.** Mount St. Helens is in Washington.

1. Marta and her cousin Pilar set up a lawn-mowing service. They made quite a bit of money over the summer. Mr. Lee was their neighbor. He had been sick lately, and his lawn had not been mowed. Marta and Pilar decided to mow the lawn for him. When Mr. Lee offered to pay them, they wouldn't take his money.

Fact	Inference		
○	○	**1. A.**	Marta and Pilar wanted to help Mr. Lee.
○	○	**B.**	Mr. Lee had been sick lately.
○	○	**C.**	Marta and Pilar were hard workers.
○	○	**D.**	Mr. Lee offered to pay the girls.

2. Popcorn is one of the oldest kinds of corn. It was first grown by people in North America and South America. Today most popcorn is grown in Nebraska and Indiana.

Fact	Inference		
○	○	**2. A.**	Popcorn is grown in Indiana.
○	○	**B.**	People in South America grew popcorn.
○	○	**C.**	Popcorn doesn't grow well everywhere.
○	○	**D.**	People still eat popcorn.

3. Dana loved computers. Once or twice a week, she went to the computer store near her house. The owner was glad to let Dana use the computers, but he told her not to bring drinks inside. One day Dana carried a can of apple juice into the store.

Fact	Inference		
○	○	**3. A.**	Dana spilled the apple juice.
○	○	**B.**	The owner was angry with Dana.
○	○	**C.**	Dana liked apple juice.
○	○	**D.**	The store was near Dana's house.

4. Mammoths lived thousands of years ago. They looked a little like elephants. They had trunks and long teeth called tusks. Some had hair all over their bodies. They were called woolly mammoths. The bones of mammoths have been found in Siberia. The last mammoths died about 10,000 years ago.

Fact	Inference	
○	○	**4. A.** Woolly mammoths had hair on their bodies.
○	○	**B.** Mammoths had trunks and tusks.
○	○	**C.** Woolly mammoths died long ago.
○	○	**D.** Mammoths lived in Siberia.

---

5. Andy watched his mother take his training wheels off. He was excited to try out his bike. Without the training wheels, he kept falling off. Then his older brother Jeff came outside. Jeff had an idea. He ran beside Andy as Andy pedaled the bike. Andy rode faster and faster. Soon Jeff couldn't keep up. Andy was riding the bike by himself!

Fact	Inference	
○	○	**5. A.** Andy fell off his bike.
○	○	**B.** Jeff wanted to help Andy.
○	○	**C.** Andy's mother took off his training wheels.
○	○	**D.** Jeff was Andy's older brother.

1. Mushrooms grow under piles of fallen leaves or on dead logs. People eat mushrooms in spaghetti or on pizza, but not all mushrooms are good to eat. Some mushrooms have poison in them. The poisonous ones are called toadstools.

Fact	Inference	
○	○	**1. A.** Some mushrooms are poisonous.
○	○	**B.** People eat mushrooms on pizza.
○	○	**C.** Mushrooms grow on dead logs.
○	○	**D.** People should not eat toadstools.

2. One man made a pizza so big it could feed 30,000 people. The pizza was more than 100 feet across. It was cut into more than 90,000 slices! The man's name was Mr. Avato. He set a world record.

Fact	Inference	
○	○	**2. A.** The pizza was more than 100 feet across.
○	○	**B.** The pizza set a world record.
○	○	**C.** Mr. Avato likes pizza.
○	○	**D.** There were more than 90,000 pieces.

3. Rob heard a rooster crow. He opened his eyes and felt the sun shining through the window. It was his first day on his cousin's farm. He jumped out of bed and began putting on his jeans. When his aunt called him to breakfast, he ran downstairs eagerly.

Fact	Inference		
○	○	**3. A.**	Rob liked farm life.
○	○	**B.**	The sun was shining.
○	○	**C.**	Rob was hungry.
○	○	**D.**	A rooster crowed.

4. Think about this the next time you brush your teeth. Before people had toothbrushes, they used twigs. They would smash the end to make it like a brush. About 600 years ago, the toothbrush was invented in China. It was made from hog hair. Hog hairs are very stiff and are called bristles. The bristles were attached to a wooden stick. Today, toothbrushes are not made with hog hairs. They have nylon bristles.

Fact	Inference		
○	○	**4. A.**	Toothbrushes have changed over time.
○	○	**B.**	People first used twigs to clean their teeth.
○	○	**C.**	Modern toothbrushes have nylon bristles.
○	○	**D.**	The first toothbrushes used wooden sticks and hog hair.

5. When we think of windmills, we often think of Holland. The people there used windmills to take water off their land. That way they had more land for farming. Now windmills are used to make electricity.

Fact	Inference		
○	○	**5. A.**	There is not enough farmland in Holland.
○	○	**B.**	Farmland must be fairly dry.
○	○	**C.**	Holland has many windmills.
○	○	**D.**	Now windmills make electricity.

1. A compass is used as a guide. The needle of a compass always points north. The needle is really just a small magnet. The needle is balanced so that it turns freely. When the compass is turned, the needle continues to point north. The compass was invented in China about 2,000 years ago. It was used to guide ships on long trips.

Fact	Inference	
○	○	**1. A.** If a compass is turned, the needle still points one direction.
○	○	**B.** A compass could help a ship when the sky is cloudy.
○	○	**C.** A compass always points north.
○	○	**D.** Ship captains found the compass helpful.

2. The Venus flytrap is a strange plant. An insect that flies near it doesn't have much of a chance. When an insect touches the leaves in the center of the plant, the leaves snap shut. The insect gets trapped inside. It takes a few days for the Venus flytrap to finish eating the insect.

Fact	Inference	
○	○	**2. A.** A Venus flytrap is a plant.
○	○	**B.** The Venus flytrap's leaves snap shut.
○	○	**C.** The leaves trap the insect.
○	○	**D.** Venus flytraps eat insects.

3. A coral reef is a strange and beautiful place. It has towers, tunnels, caves, and castles, but it is under the sea. The coral is made of shells from tiny animals. It looks like rock. Different kinds of fish swim around the reef. They make the reef look like a rainbow of color.

Fact	Inference	
○	○	**3. A.** Coral reefs are beautiful.
○	○	**B.** Fish swim around a coral reef.
○	○	**C.** The fish are colorful.
○	○	**D.** A coral reef is made of shells.

4. Koko was a gorilla. Penny, her owner, had taught the ape sign language. One day Penny asked Koko what she wanted for her birthday. "Cat," Koko answered. Penny bought a toy cat for Koko. When Koko opened her present, she threw it down. Koko had wanted a real cat. A few months later, Penny gave Koko a real cat. Then Koko was happy.

Fact	Inference	
○	○	**4. A.** Penny was Koko's owner.
○	○	**B.** Koko wanted a cat for her birthday.
○	○	**C.** The real cat made Koko happy.
○	○	**D.** Koko was upset when she didn't get a cat.

---

5. Dodo birds once lived on some islands in the Indian Ocean. They were about the same size as a turkey. Dodos could not fly. They had a hooked beak, short legs, and a short neck. Dodo eggs were eaten by other animals on the islands. The last dodos died out more than 200 years ago.

Fact	Inference	
○	○	**5. A.** A dodo was the size of a turkey.
○	○	**B.** The dodos died more than 200 years ago.
○	○	**C.** A dodo was larger than a chicken.
○	○	**D.** Other animals ate dodo eggs.

Writing Roundup

Read each story. Then read the question that follows it.
Write your answers on the lines below each question.

1. Karen watered the rose plant. It was in a pot. Then she spotted water leaking under the pot. She did not want water stains on the shelf, so she put some old newspapers under the pot. As she did this, the sun hit her and the rose. Tomorrow the rose would be in a new pot.

Where did Karen keep the flowerpot?

_____

_____

2. Leon pulled his pencil out of the sharpener. Then he shook the shavings off the pencil. It looked fine. He was ready to start writing again.

Why did Leon stop writing?

_____

_____

3. The dog looked up and down the street. The man waited until the dog stepped off the curb. Then the man followed the dog. They crossed the street.

Why did the man wait for the dog?

_____

_____

Read the paragraph below. Then answer the questions.

Mary grew 6 inches in her first year in high school. Now she wants to join the basketball team. Mary knows she must build her skills over the summer. Every day she practices her shooting and dribbling. Some days she gets her little brother to help. She practices passing the ball to him. Soon Mary plans to visit the playground. There she can practice with players who are on the team. She can learn how she is doing. She can also find out what else she needs to learn.

1. Why didn't Mary join the team in her first year?

_____

_____

2. What skill does Mary's little brother need to help Mary?

_____

_____

3. What kind of person is Mary?

_____

_____

4. How does Mary feel about her skills?

_____

_____

Check Yourself

Unit 1

What Are Facts?

p. 6

Fact: Opals are stones that sparkle with many colors.

Fact: Coober Pedy is in South Australia.

Practice Finding Facts

p. 7

3. D

Lesson 1 pp. 8–9

1. D	6. C
2. D	7. D
3. A	8. A
4. C	9. D
5. B	10. B

Lesson 2 pp. 10–11

1. C	6. D
2. B	7. D
3. C	8. D
4. D	9. B
5. B	10. D

Lesson 3 pp. 12–13

1. A	6. D
2. D	7. B
3. A	8. C
4. C	9. C
5. C	10. A

Lesson 4 pp. 14–15

1. C	6. C
2. D	7. A
3. B	8. C
4. A	9. B
5. C	10. D

Lesson 5 pp. 16–17

1. B	6. B
2. A	7. C
3. C	8. A
4. B	9. D
5. C	10. D

Lesson 6 pp. 18–19

1. C	6. C
2. D	7. D
3. B	8. D
4. A	9. B
5. D	10. A

Lesson 7 pp. 20–21

1. D	6. C
2. C	7. C
3. D	8. D
4. A	9. C
5. B	10. A

Lesson 8 pp. 22–23

1. B	6. C
2. B	7. D
3. A	8. C
4. D	9. D
5. B	10. B

Writing Roundup

p. 24

Possible answers include:

1. A comet looks like a fuzzy star with a tail.

2. The tail looks long and bright when the comet flies near the Sun.

3. Halley's Comet can be seen about every 77 years.

p. 25

Check that you have four facts in your story.

Unit 2

What Is Sequence?

p. 26

2, 1, 3

Practice with Sequence

p. 27

3. A

Lesson 1 pp. 28–29

1. 2, 3, 1
2. B
3. A
4. B
5. C

Lesson 2 pp. 30–31

1. 2, 3, 1
2. A
3. C
4. C
5. B

Lesson 3 pp. 32–33

1. 2, 1, 3
2. A
3. B
4. B
5. C

Lesson 4 pp. 34–35

1. 2, 1, 3
2. C
3. A
4. B
5. A

Lesson 5 pp. 36–37

1. 2, 3, 1
2. C
3. A
4. B
5. C

Lesson 6 pp. 38–39

1. 3, 2, 1
2. C
3. A
4. B
5. A

Lesson 7 pp. 40–41

1. 3, 1, 2
2. B
3. C
4. C
5. A

Lesson 8 pp. 42–43

1. 3, 1, 2
2. C
3. A
4. B
5. B

Writing Roundup

p. 44

Possible answers include:

1. Leo said he had a rock collection at lunch.

2. Leo smiled and thanked his friends.

3. Jonelle decided to give Leo a rock after he told her about his collection.

4. Leo opened Duane's present second.

p. 45

Check that your story is written in sequence.

Check that you have used time order words, such as first, next, and last.

Unit 3

Working with Context

p. 47
2. A
3. C

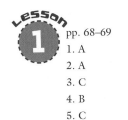

Lesson 1
pp. 48–49

1. D	9. A
2. A	10. B
3. A	11. C
4. B	12. B
5. D	13. A
6. C	14. B
7. B	15. A
8. D	16. D

Lesson 2
pp. 50–51

1. B	9. D
2. A	10. B
3. C	11. A
4. C	12. D
5. D	13. C
6. B	14. B
7. D	15. B
8. B	16. A

Lesson 3
pp. 52–53

1. B	9. D
2. D	10. A
3. A	11. A
4. C	12. C
5. D	13. B
6. B	14. D
7. D	15. C
8. A	16. A

Lesson 4
pp. 54–55

1. B	9. B
2. A	10. A
3. D	11. B
4. A	12. D
5. A	13. A
6. C	14. C
7. B	15. A
8. B	16. D

Lesson 5
pp. 56–57

1. C	5. D
2. C	6. D
3. A	7. A
4. B	8. C

Lesson 6
pp. 58–59

1. C	5. C
2. C	6. B
3. B	7. A
4. B	8. D

Lesson 7
pp. 60–61

1. A	5. A
2. B	6. C
3. A	7. B
4. D	8. D

Lesson 8
pp. 62–63

1. D	5. D
2. B	6. A
3. A	7. B
4. C	8. D

Writing Roundup

p. 64
Possible answers include:
1. wet or clean
2. dirt or mud
3. stars or moon
4. day or summer
5. class or school
6. sit or play

p. 65
Possible answers include
1. picking up litter
   or planting trees
2. the principal or the mayor
3. make a garden or plant flowers
4. the mall or his favorite store
5. a sale sign or an ad
6. a book or earrings

Unit 4

Practice Finding the Main Idea

p. 67
2. The correct answer is B. There are details about the Sahara's location, rainfall, and temperature. If you add these details together, you will get the main idea.

Lesson 1
pp. 68–69

1. A
2. A
3. C
4. B
5. C

Lesson 2
pp. 70–71

1. C
2. B
3. C
4. C
5. B

Lesson 3
pp. 72–73

1. A
2. C
3. B
4. B
5. A

Lesson 4
pp. 74–75

1. B
2. C
3. A
4. A
5. B

Lesson 5
pp. 76–77

1. A
2. B
3. C
4. B
5. A

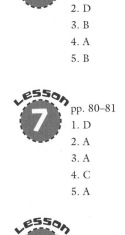

Lesson 6
pp. 78–79

1. D
2. D
3. B
4. A
5. B

Lesson 7
pp. 80–81

1. D
2. A
3. A
4. C
5. A

Lesson 8
pp. 82–83

1. A
2. C
3. B
4. D
5. A

Writing Roundup

p. 84
Possible answers include:

1. Mary Myers was the first woman balloon pilot.

2. Beto is a famous jockey because he learned to ride horses at his uncle's farm.

3. There's still a lot to learn about oceans.

p. 85

Check that you have underlined your main idea.

Check that you have used three details in your story.

Unit 5

Using What You Know

p. 87

zebra, elephant, giraffe, dolphin

LESSON 1 pp. 88–89
1. B
2. C
3. C
4. C
5. A

LESSON 2 pp. 90–91
1. C
2. A
3. C
4. B
5. A

LESSON 3 pp. 92–93
1. A
2. A
3. C
4. C
5. C

LESSON 4 pp. 94–95
1. C
2. D
3. A
4. B
5. D

LESSON 5 pp. 96–97
1. C
2. D
3. C
4. A
5. B

LESSON 6 pp. 98–99
1. D
2. C
3. A
4. B
5. C

LESSON 7 pp. 100–101
1. B
2. A
3. C
4. A
5. D

LESSON 8 pp. 102–103
1. B
2. D
3. A
4. D
5. C

Writing Roundup

p. 104

Possible answers include:

1. Movies didn't always have talking.

2. The English family's goldfish was at least 43 years old.

3. Most people who see the Super Bowl watch it on television.

p. 105

Possible answers include:

1. Raul was not born in America. He came to America from Cuba.

2. Raul did not meet his granduncle in Cuba. He found out about his granduncle after he moved to Florida.

3. Raul and his mom don't live alone. They live with Raul's granduncle.

4. Raul probably doesn't want to move back to Florida. He thinks he will like New Jersey.

Unit 6

LESSON 1 pp. 108–109
1. B
2. C
3. D
4. A
5. A

LESSON 2 pp. 110–111
1. A
2. C
3. C
4. D
5. C

LESSON 3 pp. 112–113
1. D
2. B
3. A
4. A
5. A

LESSON 4 pp. 114–115
1. B
2. D
3. A
4. C
5. A

LESSON 5 pp. 116–117
1. A. F B. I
   C. F D. F
2. A. I B. F
   C. F D. I
3. A. F B. I
   C. I D. F
4. A. I B. I
   C. I D. F
5. A. F B. I
   C. I D. F

LESSON 6 pp. 118–119
1. A. I B. F
   C. I D. F
2. A. F B. F
   C. I D. I

3. A. I B. I
   C. I D. F
4. A. F B. F
   C. F D. I
5. A. F B. F
   C. F D. F

LESSON 7 pp. 120–121
1. A. F B. F
   C. F D. I
2. A. F B. F
   C. I D. F
3. A. I B. F
   C. I D. F
4. A. I B. F
   C. F D. F
5. A. I B. I
   C. I D. F

LESSON 8 pp. 122–123
1. A. F B. I
   C. F D. I
2. A. F B. F
   C. F D. F
3. A. F B. F
   C. I D. F
4. A. F B. F
   C. F D. I
5. A. F B. F
   C. I D. F

Writing Roundup

p. 124
Possible answers include:

1. Karen kept the pot on a shelf next to a window.

2. Leon's pencil needed sharpening.

3. The dog was a guide dog or Seeing Eye dog.

p. 125
Possible answers include:

1. She thought she wasn't tall enough. She didn't think she played well enough.

2. He needs to be able to catch passes.

3. Mary is willing to learn, hard-working, and serious.

4. Mary is not certain about her skills. She seems to think she has more to learn.